Navigating Change

Global Health, AIDS, CDC & the United Nations

BY DEBORAH L. RUGG, PHD

Navigating Change

Global Health, AIDS, CDC & the United Nations

DEBORAH L. RUGG, PHD

StoryTerrace

Text Deborah L. Rugg, PhD
Design Mitar Stjepcevic, on behalf of StoryTerrace
Copyright © Deborah L. Rugg, PhD

All rights reserved. This book or parts thereof may not be reproduced in any form, stored in any retrieval system, or transmitted in any form by any means—electronic, mechanical, photocopy, recording, or otherwise—without prior written permission of the publisher, except as provided by United States of America copyright law.

First print May 2022

StoryTerrace

www.StoryTerrace.com

CONTENTS

ACKNOWLEDGMENTS	7
FOREWORD	9
1. FIGHTING A PANDEMIC	13
2. TAKING FLIGHT	25
3. DISCOVERING MY PASSION	43
4. EMERGING CRISIS	57
5. FAMILY TRANSITIONS	69
6. CULTURE SHOCK	77
7. ADVERSARIES TO ALLIES	91
8. PANDEMIC SCIENCE, MYTHS AND HEROES	99
9. SPRINGBOARD FROM SETBACKS	111
10. WORLD STAGE	121
11. MAKING A DIFFERENCE	139
12. ART OF DIPLOMACY	153
13. TAKING A NEW TACK	171
14. FULL CIRCLE	185
DEDICATION	195
ABOUT THE AUTHOR	197
SUGGESTED READINGS	201

ACKNOWLEDGMENTS

My long journey in writing this memoir has had many twists and turns, and many people provided me with critical support along the way. I would like to acknowledge those who encouraged me from the very start to write my stories down, and were also there at the very end, still cheering me on. I would also like to thank all those at StoryTerrace who helped me make this last push across the finish line and get it published.

First and foremost, I would like to acknowledge and thank Dr. Michael Quinn Patton, the Founder of Utilization-focused Evaluation, who wrote the forward to this book. Michael encouraged me to dive deep in writing this memoir, taking an auto-ethnographic look at what I had experienced as a female going through the social changes in my personal life and the cultural transitions in my professional career.

I would also like to acknowledge the lasting inspiration and encouragement I received early on from John Perkins, author of the NY times best-selling book "Confessions of an Economic Hitman". John said "always be clear why you are writing this book and then, just write from your heart… everything else will fall into place." He was so right. When

I lost sight of this, I struggled. When I remembered it, everything indeed quickly fell into place.

    I would like to offer my sincerest gratitude to my daughters Marisa, for her editorial acumen through several versions of the book, especially with regard to the millennials' perspectives on the issues I was raising, and Ilse, for her editorial assistance and contributing the wonderful cover photo and several photos in the book.

    All of the above helped me focus on my primary intended audience of young professionals, especially young women in the fields of public health, evaluation, and behavioral and social sciences, who themselves are facing similar challenges to what I faced juggling family and career and coming up through the ranks of academia, large organizations like the CDC and the UN, and as an entrepreneur starting my own business.

FOREWORD

Effective leaders observe, listen, reflect, learn, and guide. Global leaders do this on a global scale. Deborah Rugg is such a leader. Her observations and reflections tell us not just about the past but provide astute and insightful guidance about our collective future. Her experiences as an epidemiologist on the frontlines of the HIV/AIDS epidemic take us inside the intersection of politics, culture, and science. The mantra and admonition to "follow the science," so prevalent in the Coronavirus pandemic, originated in efforts to influence policy and practice for HIV prevention and treatment. Insights into the politicization of science abound as her personal experiences reveal the tragic consequences of scientific ignorance, political cowardice, and cultural resistance to facing the truth. Yet truth eventually prevails as the scientific narrative becomes infused into political and cultural stories through the persistence and dedication of those like Deborah Rugg, who generate and communicate real-world realities despite massive resistance to facing those realities. She writes: "A virus loves nothing more than when humans stick their heads in the sand, and society's inability to discuss sexual issues back in those days created so much unnecessary harm."

NAVIGATING CHANGE

She spent 30 years fighting the AIDS pandemic throughout the world. She takes us through the twists and turns of the battle against AIDS. In so doing she skillfully and reflectively generates lessons and insights about the role of science in society and the experience of being a scientist. Let me offer a sample of the questions the book answers. If the answers to these questions interest and intrigue you, as they did me, then you'll find this book a page-turner due both to the quality of the writing and the ongoing relevance of her story to our times.

What was it like to be a young female behavioral epidemiologist in a male-dominated medical world? What was working at the CDC like when HIV emerged? How did the CDC respond? What happened at a three-day meeting in Rome when this young female epidemiologist was sent to provide technical assistance to the Roman Catholic Church leadership as they formulated a religious stance on HIV prevention for their roughly 1 billion adherents?

When her daughter is conducting research on the disease risks of human sexual behaviors, what does a mother raised in an era when such things were not talked about tell her friends? The answer opens up the larger question of how to talk about what people don't want to talk about. And how is being involved in and committed to the all-consuming, life and-death struggle against the ravages of AIDS combined with being herself, a wife, and mother?

NAVIGATING CHANGE

These are just a few more of the many things you'll learn on this important and compelling autoethnographic journey. What is internalized homophobia and its consequences? What happens when male healthcare providers interact with gay men in a homophobic way? Why did CDC study "men who have sex with men" to avoid using the term "gay" or "homosexual"? And what differences or similarities in pandemic responses did she observe in countries around the globe? Especially inspiring are stories of the courage and tenacity of the frontline healthcare workers we meet.

You'll learn how Deborah transitioned from being a health psychologist to epidemiologist to becoming an effective and well-respected global leader in the emergent profession of program evaluation. She takes us inside how the United Nations, against enormous political odds, came to recognize the importance of evaluation, the need for strengthening evaluation capacity in the developing world, and the year 2015 as the International Year of Evaluation. Deborah helped lead that effort and important subsequent work in operationalizing indicators and the evaluation principles guiding the Sustainable Development Goals (SDGs) which constitute the world's aspirations articulated in the global sustainable development agenda for 2030.

The book concludes with advice to young people, especially young women, on managing a professional career in a way that fulfills a personal commitment to making the world a better place. The advice offered is hard-won, grounded in overcoming daunting obstacles, thus deeply authentic, and yet graced with humility and a deep caring about both individual people and the fate of humanity. The first person I'll give this book to is my own daughter.

Michael Quinn Patton, PhD
Founder of Utilization-Focused Evaluation

1

FIGHTING A PANDEMIC

It is good to have an end to journey toward; but it is the journey that matters in the end. - Ursula K. Le Guin

On a sunny day in 1991, I stepped from an airplane and onto the troubled land of Botswana. It was my first trip to Africa in the fight against AIDS (Acquired Immune Deficiency Syndrome). I felt anxious and determined to make a difference.

Immediately I admired Botswana's harsh, barren beauty. The vast Kalahari Desert made up 70 percent of this country, and you could drive for miles without seeing signs of human activity. Despite a population of just 1.3 million, Botswana had become the epicenter of Africa's rapidly escalating AIDS epidemic. My employer, the CDC (Centers for Disease Control and Prevention), needed me to evaluate the local prevention efforts.

After checking in to the Gaborone Sun Hotel, I walked to the nearest grocery store for supplies. Foolishly I bought more than I could carry and emerged from the store struggling with two huge bags. A smiling young man approached. He introduced himself. "Hello ma'am, my name is John. Do you need some help? I would be happy to help you carry your bags." Taken by his big, radiant, and warm smile, I immediately felt the kindness of his offer and accepted. While we walked, John spoke of his family and the tremendous pride he felt at being a student at the local university. As he spoke, I felt a deep sense of how truly happy and grateful he was for his loved ones, his meager possessions, his life, and the opportunity to attend school. These are all things people often take for granted where I'm from . . . until there is a crisis. Even though the AIDS epidemic was raging in his country, John seemed truly free from the deep anxieties so common in the developed world, especially during a pandemic, which I surely would have felt if I were in his situation.

As I listened, my typical Western image of poor people in Africa evaporated. John was not bitter about living in poverty or about watching so many of his family members die from inadequate healthcare. This young man was simply happy to be alive, reveling in the smallest opportunity each day gave him, such as the chance to meet me and learn about the outside world. John's buoyant outlook enriched him with a kind of peace I'd never seen before, although I'd certainly see it again while fighting the Human Immunodeficiency Virus (HIV), the cause of AIDS, in distant corners of the earth.

NAVIGATING CHANGE

Botswana's Ministry of Health assigned me an outreach worker, a young woman named Eleanora, to shepherd me around the country. From day one, Eleanora worked tirelessly by my side, arranging interviews and helping with data collection. We developed a natural work rhythm that quickly blossomed into friendship.

Eleanora was barely 23 years old, a strong and capable young woman with a lot of responsibilities, yet always a warm smile and engaging laugh. She was like John, one of the lucky ones to have received a good education in this country. We sat in the back of a sport utility vehicle, discussing the government's new school-based AIDS and sex education program, as our driver navigated the bumpy roads of the Kalahari. This was the land of the San peoples, the native nomadic tribes of Nelson Mandela's ancestors. It was stark and unforgiving, and while looking out the dusty window I decided to broach a personal subject with Eleanora: her own sexual history.

I knew she was already the mother of three and had inherited three more children from her older sister, who died of AIDS two years earlier. Eleanora's village sat about twenty miles from her downtown Gaborone workplace. Like most people she had no vehicle, or even a bike, which meant walking or taking the bus. The public buses, when running, were dirty and overcrowded. They were also notoriously unsafe for young women, especially after dark.

NAVIGATING CHANGE

Gently, I asked Eleanora about the sexual advances of men on the buses.

Right away, she became uncharacteristically shy. I noticed her hand curl into a tight little ball on the seat. Clearly, thinking about the bus upset her. I reached out and placed my hand on her fist.

"Are you OK? You can talk to me, Eleanora, if you want to." For a moment she wavered, then shook her head. "No. But thank you."

"OK," I said, "I'm here if you change your mind." And then I offered well-meaning but very insensitive advice, "You know you can always go talk anonymously at one of the HIV counseling and testing sites." Of course she already knew this, how presumptuous of me to think otherwise.

She smiled and nodded, but my eagerness to help had overwhelmed her. It was a novice mistake, one typical of well-meaning Americans who show up for the first time in a developing country thinking we have all the answers. In the awkward silence I vowed to be more sensitive and be a better listener in the future; curbing my tendency to always give advice.

The next day we visited a school district near Eleanora's village, and afterward she graciously invited me to her home, a simple, four-room structure with dirt floors. She retrieved her children from a neighbor and beamed with pride as she introduced each one. It was such a happy moment, and I stood there in awe of this cheerful young woman who always worked so hard and overcame hardships.

My time in-country ended, and we said a tearful farewell. I told her to keep up the good work. If Botswana were to survive this epidemic, it would be on the shoulders of people like her. During the flight home that day, I realized Eleanora had become my inspiration for fighting AIDS globally. She'd be the person I thought of whenever I felt too overwhelmed to continue.

A little over six months later I was back in Botswana, this time to evaluate the new World Health Organization (WHO) HIV counseling and testing protocols. Naturally, my first order of business at the Ministry of Health was to inquire about Eleanora so we could reconnect. The reply I received floored me. They said Eleanora unfortunately had died. She had died of AIDS.

I couldn't believe she was gone, or how quickly the disease had taken her. She must have already been infected when I met her the first time, though she never let on. Just six months earlier Eleanora had been a beacon of hope, energetic and completely dedicated to her job and her children. Now only orphans remained. Eleanora had died because she wasn't permitted to refuse sex. In her culture at the time, women didn't have the right to say no. For an American like me it was difficult to understand. I went to my hotel room and cried. Then I telephoned a friend back home.

NAVIGATING CHANGE

"We are losing a whole generation of young people in Africa," I cried into the staticky line. "We have to do something about this!" This was an increasingly common refrain early in the pandemic.

Of course, it wasn't just Africa. By this time, HIV had already prowled the planet for a decade. I interviewed some of its first victims back in 1981. By 1991, the disease had claimed more than 100,000 American lives and untold numbers worldwide. Alarmingly, the statistics were still trending sharply upward.

AIDS didn't just prey on the poor or marginalized. It claimed the life of Hollywood film star Rock Hudson in 1985. Hudson had been good friends with President Ronald Reagan, who took office just as the epidemic was getting started. The ultra-conservative president ignored this mounting crisis. It wasn't until the death of his dear friend—some four years after the epidemic began—that Reagan publicly uttered the word AIDS. His administration remained indifferent to the "gay plague."

Infections continued to spread like wildfire in the gay community. It wasn't until November 1991, when basketball star Earvin "Magic" Johnson announced he was HIV positive, that the rest of the country became alarmed. Two weeks later Freddie Mercury, lead singer of the rock band Queen, died of AIDS-related complications. And when an eleven-year-old boy from Indiana, Ryan White, became the first case among hemophiliacs to die from the disease, the

U.S. Congress kicked into gear with the Ryan White Care Act. Humanity was in an all-out war with this pernicious little retrovirus. From my view, out on the front lines, we were losing.

I would spend three decades of my life fighting the virus, but the funny thing is I hadn't gone into public health because of AIDS. In fact, my first interest was in health psychology and cardiovascular disease prevention. This stemmed, in part, from my father's smoking addiction and desire to understand health risk behavior so I might help him and others. But I guess the universe had other plans for me. So, in 1981, it was by coincidence that I was earning my PhD in health psychology at the University of California San Francisco (UCSF) Medical School when the first signs of trouble hit. Mysterious cases were pouring into San Francisco General and UCSF hospitals. Back then, we had no idea how the disease operated or even what to call it. We only knew that it was deadly and spreading rapidly across the city's gay community.

My early AIDS work earned me an invitation in 1987 to join the CDC's Epidemic Intelligence Service, where I became the first health psychologist to complete the rigorous two-year epidemiology training program. At the CDC, I was often the youngest participant in critical meetings, and almost always the only behavioral scientist in what I saw as "a sea of brilliant, courageous, yet rather dogmatic physicians." Later in my career, while working for the secretary general of the United Nations, I was sometimes the only American in the room, which brought its own set of complications. In many of the places I worked throughout my career, I was either the only woman, or one of just a few.

My position as a relative outsider taught me to be creative and strategic. I learned to recruit allies and build consensus from behind the scenes. I came to see adversity not as a setback, but as a springboard to success. I gained the wisdom to realize when I'd reached a dead end, which enabled me to back away and head in a different, more fruitful direction. Most of all, I learned that a motivated individual could make a lasting impact on the world. All that is needed is resilience, knowing when to walk away, and when to "take the bull by horns."

Young people today, especially young women, face the same challenges I did some 40 years ago. Much has changed, of course, but not enough, and many organizations remain the dominion of men. We still have inequality of pay. The Me Too movement showed that sexual harassment remains a workplace scourge. Many young mothers are expected to take on the bulk of parenting duties while still managing a full-time career.

My advice to you is to never ever give up. Women can survive and even thrive in such demanding environments, though admittedly it is not easy. I overcame the hurdles slowly, via trial and error, with the help of friends and allies, a growing resilience, sense of purpose, and determination to achieve my goals.

During the course of my career, I have had the opportunity to work in more than 100 countries. Along the way I met some fascinating people and witnessed amazing sights. I enjoyed wonderful colleagues who shared in my efforts to influence public policy on a national and global scale. My hope in writing this book is that you will gain insights from my successes and my failures and see that one woman truly can make a difference in this world. And so can you.

My life so far has been an incredible journey, one that I am delighted to share with you. It begins in rural Wisconsin, where I learned my first lessons in leadership, resilience, and speaking my truth.

National Health Institute, Gaborone, Botswana (l-r) head nurse, me, lead HIV outreach worker, my host, Eleanora, 1991.

Me, Eleanora- an HIV outreach worker- her sons & sister's daughters on my first trip to Gaborone, Botswana in 1991.

2

TAKING FLIGHT

Adventure is worthwhile in itself. - Amelia Earhart

My father was a Navy man. Duane Austin Rugg served in the Korean Conflict from 1950–1954 on board a ship stationed first in the Mediterranean Sea. Afterwards the Navy sent him to Puerto Rico, where he was joined by his high school sweetheart, Beverly Marie Revor. They married and started a family, beginning with me, born on March 3, 1953, in San Juan.

The young family returned to Wisconsin after Dad completed his military service. In time I would have two brothers, Jerry and Steve, and a sister, Sue. We lived in the town of Schofield and spent many summer days with my Aunt Darlene and Uncle Harvey, who owned a picturesque dairy farm in Chippewa Falls. On the farm everyone earned their keep, including the children. I remember getting up at sunrise every day for a big farm breakfast before heading off to help milk the cows, clean their stalls, and load my Uncle Harvey's milk truck. Some mornings were particularly exciting when he would say, "Debbie, would you like to join me on my milk route this morning?" Squealing with delight, I always said, "Yes I would!"

In addition to sitting up front in the cab, I got to tag along as he collected the milk cans from the other farms and unloaded them at the local dairy. I watched in amazement how milk was pasteurized and made into that famous Wisconsin cheddar cheese from the milk we delivered! Once our chores were done, and the cows were out of the barn, we were completely free to explore the rolling corn fields and vast woodlands all day long until it was time for dinner. I grew up as a bit of a tomboy, and in those early days I could be found exploring, riding horses, herding cows, getting eggs from the chicken coop for breakfast, honey from the beehives, and watching baby farm animals be born. Witnessing how a baby calf is born is quite a memorable sight.

I believe my early resilience and self-reliance really got its start during these endless summer days. We (my brother Jerry and cousins Gary, Mark, David, and Daniel, teasingly called Daniel Boone or Boone) reveled in our imaginations and the adventure stories of Huckleberry Finn and Tom Sawyer. I was the oldest in my family, and second oldest among my 21 cousins. My mom was the oldest too. I came from a long line of first-born females, I was told. Further adventure awaited us kids at Lake Chetek, where my family had a cottage. I recall many happy days there as well, water skiing while my dad drove the boat, fishing and telling stories

NAVIGATING CHANGE

with my grandfather, frying the fish we caught that day (mostly Lake Perch or Sunfish) for dinner with my mother, and playing cards and laughing with my grandmother until bedtime. We would catch so much fish over the summer, we could take it home, freeze it, and have enough to eat at our Friday Night Fish Fry the rest of the year. Being raised Catholic, we did not eat meat on Fridays.

Dad's naval aviation skills earned him a job as an air traffic controller at our local airport. The small facility grew quiet during his midnight shifts, which Dad called "workin' the mids," so sometimes he invited me along. I would grab my sleeping bag and Mom would pack me a snack and excitedly off I would go. I would then play on the floor in his office while he worked, making sure to stay out of his way. I enjoyed scribbling with a grease pen on the wall sized maps and listening to the mechanical chatter of the teletype machine. I particularly remember one Christmas Eve when I was about eight. I joined Dad for a few hours at work. It was one of my most memorable times because that night he showed me some exciting news that had just come across the teletype machine. The Federal Aviation Administration (FAA) had just reported an unusual sighting of flying reindeer pulling what seemed to be a man in a sleigh. I now had all the proof I needed; Santa Claus was real!

I also fondly remember the times we'd go outside so Dad could release a helium balloon to test the cloud ceiling. Afterwards, we'd breathe the helium from the balloon, laughing hysterically as we both sounded like Donald Duck when we talked.

Typically, Dad was very strict with us kids, but he had a big heart and we always knew he loved us. I can remember him being remarkably kind to strangers, particularly those in need. At the movies he teared up when the hero died, especially if it was a Western or war movie. He always said to judge people by their actions and their character, which was good advice I never forgot.

More than once at the airport I saw Dad take control of a life-threatening situation when an aircraft had gotten itself into trouble. In a reassuring voice, Dad fed the distressed pilot vital information and instructions, and talked him down. Even as a child, peeking from an office doorway, I sensed the situation's gravity. People's lives were at stake. Most of all, I perceived Dad's leadership. His tone said: "Don't worry. I'm going to guide you to safety." And that's exactly what he did, every time. Leaders stay calm when others panic, I realized. They think through the problem and implement a solution. Watching Dad made me proud. I wanted to be a leader, too.

By the time I was twelve, I had lost interest in the farm and the cottage. Friends, school, and social gatherings mattered more to me now. I did a lot of reading and began forming opinions about social injustices in the world, such as communist rule and America's rapidly escalating war in

NAVIGATING CHANGE

Vietnam. My childhood innocence had given way to greater intellectual growth, and I liked it.

I was attending public school but being raised Catholic, which meant mandatory attendance at Saturday morning religion classes. They called it the Confraternity of Christian Doctrine, or CCD, and I had never minded attending the classes. At least until recently, when some of the teachings started to bother me. The CCD nuns always spoke in absolutes. In their eyes, people were either good or bad, faithful or sinful. I knew it had to be far more complex than that, but I didn't say anything.

Finally, the issue came to a head one Saturday morning, when a nun delivered a long lecture about what happens when we die. She stated flatly that unbaptized babies go to limbo and unbaptized adults go to hell.

"That can't be right," I blurted out.

I suddenly felt the eyes of all my classmates. The nun told me to stand up.

"They can't all go to hell just for being unbaptized," I said. "The way you are teaching this sounds to me more like the way communism is taught. I am having a hard time buying it anymore. It seems much more complicated than this."

She scowled and told me to go wait in the hallway. I trudged out, my footsteps echoing through the quiet room, and I sat down on the hall floor. Fifteen minutes later my parents showed up to get me, and we drove home in silence. I sat at the kitchen table while they spoke privately in the den. I fidgeted as my emotions bounced between fear and defiance.

Finally, Dad called me into the den.

"Debbie, I just can't believe you these days. What's gotten into you? You are grounded for a month." Dad was unhappy with the disrespect I had shown, but didn't try to defend the nun. I assumed this was because he was a Methodist. I stormed off and pouted in my room. Clearly it was wrong of me to be so disrespectful to the nun, but my beliefs still felt right. During the long month that followed, I came to realize being right wasn't always enough. I had experienced my first encounter with the need for diplomacy when speaking my truth.

As I moved into my early teens, my father and I grew further apart. I was changing in ways he didn't understand, and sometimes I didn't either. His only solution for dealing with a teenage girl was to provide more discipline, which only fueled my rebellious streak. Despite the clashes, Dad tried his best to keep our special connection alive, and for that I was grateful even if I didn't show it.

One day he took me to the airport for a ride in a Cessna, which was terribly exciting as I had never flown before. All of our family trips had been by car. The little plane zipped down the runway and climbed into a lustrous blue sky like a "homesick angel," which is what Dad always called airplanes when they were taking off. We leveled off, and then to my great surprise, he asked if I wanted to take the controls. It was a gesture of confidence and his acknowledgment that I was growing up. Excitedly I wrapped my hands around the yoke and pulled back. We began a steep climb.

"Whoa," he said. "Push it forward a little."

I fully extended my arms, throwing us into a hair-raising dive, but Dad remained calm as always. He explained that good pilots make gradual changes, letting the aircraft respond before going any further. Soon I understood the subtleties of straight and level flight. As the lush Wisconsin countryside scrolled beneath us, I enjoyed the sensation of flying with and against the wind and the fascinating lightness of touch that controlled such a powerful machine.

For the rest of my life, I would adore flying in small aircraft, taking every opportunity to relive the freedom I felt during that first flight with Dad. I've since sat in the cockpits for many awe-inspiring flights. Once over Mount Everest on Buddha Air out of Kathmandu, Nepal. Once during a visit to Kenya and Tanzania, on a game flight realizing my lifelong dream of aerial observation of the mass migration of wildebeest and zebra in the Serengeti, where I got to "buzz a million wildebeests!" I'll never forget those amazing sights and panoramic views of nature's incredible beauty.

By my senior year of high school, I was flexing my wings as a budding leader as I became the senior class president, president of the American Field Service student exchange program, a homecoming queen candidate, and local Kiwanis Club Girl of the Month. The Vietnam War preoccupied my thoughts as well. My clash with the CCD nun had faded into distant memory. I went through the motions of my Catholic upbringing, knowing that someday I could choose to leave it all behind. However, that day would not arrive anytime soon. As it turned out, I'd be getting another dose of Catholicism, and it would be quite a heavy one. My great aunt was a nun who happened to teach at Mount Mary College in Milwaukee. She ensured the scholarship committee received a copy of my high school transcript and based on my grades they offered me a generous scholarship. I was flattered but also reluctant. Aside from being Catholic, Mount Mary enrolled only women. An all-female religious school did not sound like the most exciting college experience.

My parents sat me down in the den. It was a good school, they said, noting that scholarships were rare. My father's job always provided well for our family, but the fact remained that, in this era, air traffic controllers were grossly underpaid. They made a compelling argument, and with some hesitancy I agreed. After all, living in Milwaukee had to be more exciting than living in Schofield. In the fall of 1971, I set off for my freshman year.

It went as poorly as you might imagine. Right from the start, I challenged my professors on matters of philosophy and evolution. I railed against the Vatican's stance on family planning and abortion. To their credit, the professors gave me more leeway to argue than had the CCD nun, but clearly I was an outsider at Mount Mary.

NAVIGATING CHANGE

I had been right about Milwaukee being more exciting than Schofield, except it seemed only students at other colleges were having fun. Mount Mary imposed a strict curfew and a dorm-wide ban on male visitors. On Saturdays, my friends and I would have to head back to our sleepy campus just as the fun in town was getting started. I began sneaking out at night and missing curfew to go to parties with my new boyfriend, Tom, a Marquette University student.

After just one semester, my parents and I had another sit down in the den. They knew I was miserable at Mount Mary and gave me permission to transfer. I immediately switched to the University of Wisconsin–Milwaukee, taking summer classes at the UW-Madison campus. Madison was particularly liberating at the time. I finally felt I could breathe and live life by my own rules, not someone else's.

Another transformation occurred. I had begun my college career studying liberal arts, but soon I found myself drawn to the sciences. The scientific method spoke to me. I wanted answers to the big questions in life, such as how we came to be and how our minds function. In particular, the mind-body relationship fascinated me. I wanted to understand how our consciousness bridges itself with the physical world. In 1975, I graduated from college with a degree in physiological psychology. I immediately applied to graduate school in California and was accepted at San Diego State University's program in experimental psychology. My parents assumed I would settle down, get married, have children, and stay nearby, but that just wasn't in the cards. I tossed my belongings into the back of a U-Haul truck and climbed into the cab with two friends.

As the big truck rumbled out of town and headed west on the open highways to California, I felt a rush of exhilaration sweep over my body unlike anything I had ever experienced. I knew I was on the right path. Wisconsin had been an ideal place to grow up, but now I was ready to see what else was out there.

NAVIGATING CHANGE

Mom & Dad, married while Dad was in the Navy in San Juan, Puerto Rico, January, 1952.

NAVIGATING CHANGE

Me around 2 years, northern Wisconsin, 1955.

NAVIGATING CHANGE

Me at 4 at my grandparents house in Chippewa Falls, WI, 1957.

At home in 1960, Schofield, WI: Dad, brother Jerry, 5 (left of Dad); sister Sue, 4 (center), neighbors and me (far right) at age 7.

D.C. Everest High School Graduation. Don Alexejun, football quarterback & me, senior class president, Schofield, WI 1971.

NAVIGATING CHANGE

For Kiwanis
Deborah Rugg is girl of the month

Deborah Rugg, a senior at D. C. Everest High School, has been named Kiwanis girl of the month for May.

Deborah, the daughter of Mr. and Mrs. Duane Rugg, 1811 Daley Ave., Schofield, is president of her class and the American Field Service chapter at D. C. Everest. A school newspaper reporter, Deborah is a member of the student council, German Club, debate, intramurals, homecoming court, prom court, annual staff chairman of the winter formal and member of that court.

During her previous high schoolyears, Deborah was treasurer of the AFS, a school newspaper reporter, a member of the student council, German Club, pep band, prom committee, intramurals, and music festival. She was freshman class secretary and a cheerleader that year.

She also is a four-year member of the Ski and Pep Clubs and the Girls Athletic Association.

Deborah organized the recent forum for Government Day. She is on the governing board of the Young Adult Center and is active in its operation and fund raising. She is chairman of the Young Democrats at D. C. Everest and has worked during recent elections in canvassing.

An active Girl Scout for three years, Deborah is a member of St. Therese Catholic Church, Rothschild, and was a member of the youth organization there. She participates in Confraternity of Christian Doctrine (CCD) classes and has helped with the church fair stand.

Deborah worked part-time in a local supermarket until recently and will work this summer at a resort. She lists reading, painting, snow and water skiing as her hobbies.

Deborah plans to attend Mount Mary College, Milwaukee, and major in philosophy and speech.

She and her parents were honored Thursday evening at the Elks Club during the regular meeting of the Kiwanis Club of Greater Wausau. She received a corsage, an engraved Kiwanis charm bracelet and a certificate of achievement.

Deborah also received a check for $25 from the D. C. Everest AFS chapter.

The Kiwanis program, which began in January 1964, will terminate its activities until October, when the 69th girl of the month will be selected.

...Payne photo
DEBORAH RUGG

Wausau Daily Herald article about receiving Kiwanis Club Girl of the Month Award, May 1971.

NAVIGATING CHANGE

My maternal grandmother Theresa Revor, me, my Great Aunt Sister Remy & Mom at Mount Mary College, Milwaukee, WI, Sept., 1971.

Me at 21, University of Wisconsin, Milwaukee, WI, 1975.

3

DISCOVERING MY PASSION

When you do things from your soul, you feel a river moving you along, a joy. - Rumi

I spent a month in Los Angeles before going down to San Diego State University (SDSU). The laid-back California lifestyle fit me perfectly, and I quickly embraced yoga, meditation, Eastern philosophy, and vegetarianism. I had a tall, blond, longhaired boyfriend named Steve and a brindle Great Dane named Karma.

The boyfriend was OK, but Karma and I became inseparable. She even went to class with me, where she became an unofficial mascot of the graduate psychology program. I threw myself into my studies, learning experimental research methods and conducting behavior modification therapy with hyperactive children. The work was fascinating, and I was helping kids. Nothing could have been better.

Outside of school, I met a 65-year-old woman named Agnes who simply blew my mind. Agnes was an independent free thinker who had been an Army nurse in World War II and later became an inventor with three patents. She spoke three languages and had raised a total of fifteen orphans. She lived in the desert, on a swath of property just one half mile from the Mexican border, in the small town of Dulzura, California.

Agnes had a large garage in need of repair, and she had placed an ad on the SDSU student housing and jobs board. I was looking for an affordable housing situation and called her immediately. She said my boyfriend and I could live there for virtually nothing if we helped her fix it up. Dulzura sat 40 miles inland from San Diego and the Pacific Coast, which meant a long commute to school, and to town, but we agreed. It proved an excellent decision. Agnes taught us so much about being self-sufficient and self-reliant. It was a shockingly fun "hippie back-to-nature" period of my life I will always remember fondly. (In fact, recently my girlfriends from Seattle, Jane and Vicki, and I took a spa vacation to Rancho La Puerta Resort in Tecate, Mexico, adjacent to Mt. Kuchuma across the border from Dulzura. Wonderful and intensely vivid memories all came flooding back like it was yesterday.)

Agnes taught us basic plumbing, carpentry, and electrical work, as well as gardening and animal husbandry. In fact I cared for a nanny goat and two small billy goats and felt like I was back on my uncle's Wisconsin dairy farm. We learned to make small batches of goat milk and cheese and sold it at the local community market under the brand name Ruggmill Dairy, with the corny but catchy slogan "No udders better!" At school, I was conducting my master's thesis on the role of electro-myograph (EMG) biofeedback in treating migraines. It involved attaching electrodes to a person's head, neck, and hands. My subjects were aviators from Naval Air Station Miramar, known today as home of the U.S. Navy Fighter Weapons School or TOPGUN. The goal was to help pilots control their stress headaches during prolonged air exercises. As before, the work was fascinating. During this period, I spent a lot of time thinking about my father. He had started smoking as a young man in the Navy, and in the subsequent decades, nicotine had only tightened its grip on his life. He had made a few attempts at quitting over the years, but job stress always drove him back to the comfort of cigarettes. By the late 1970s, new studies were showing an undeniable connection between tobacco use and heart attacks. I shared the data with Dad, but he refused to quit or even cut back on his pack-and-a-half daily habit. The real eye-opener about his addiction came when my mother outlawed smoking in the house. A mere inconvenience in summer, it would become a hardship during the frigid Wisconsin winters. No doubt my mother hoped he'd eventually give up cigarettes just to stay warm, but Dad would not be denied. He set up a space heater in the garage and slipped out there whenever nicotine called to him. In time he insulated the entire garage, transforming it into a fully stocked workshop (he was always fixing or building something and had every tool imaginable, at least to me) and a cozy spot to smoke. I desperately wanted to help him quit.

Of course, it wasn't just Dad. At the time, four in ten American adults smoked, resulting in hundreds of thousands of premature deaths each year from cancer, respiratory illness, and heart disease. I wanted to join the fight against this national health crisis by helping people to quit smoking. First, I wanted to dig deeper into the mind-body connection and better understand the physiological and psychological roots of addiction.

It so happened that the University of California, San Francisco (UCSF) School of Medicine was launching the nation's first doctoral program in health psychology. This new field of study would "apply psychological theories, principles, and research to the understanding of physical health and well-being." I immediately applied, scarcely believing my luck, and then nervously awaited a reply. The trailblazing program had just a few slots available, meaning competition would be fierce.

Three months passed without a response; I had just about abandoned all hope when a UCSF envelope arrived in my mailbox. With trembling fingers, I quickly opened it. After reading the first sentence, I knew it was an acceptance letter and squealed with delight. The universe had laid out the perfect career path for me. I just needed to take that first step. So I packed up my meager belongings and moved to the ever-exotic city by the Bay, San Francisco, in the summer of 1977.

During the next few years, I delved into the troubling world of cardiovascular risk behavior and tobacco addiction. I directed projects funded by the National Heart, Lung, and Blood Institute, at the Langley Porter Psychiatric Institute at UCSF. With my colleague Sharon, we would develop and evaluate innovative smoking cessation interventions. We performed rigorous randomized controlled trials, where we assigned groups of people to a variety of intervention methods. Our interventions even included aversive conditioning, where participants puffed cigarettes so rapidly that they became ill and felt like vomiting. Where most methods had underwhelming results, our Relapse Prevention Method, which blended behavior modification and conditioning, seemed to be a promising exception.

My research won the UCSF Department of Psychiatry Robert E. Harris Memorial Award for Outstanding Research in Psychology in 1981. It challenged conventional wisdom about psychosocial and gender differences in risk behaviors and quitting smoking. For example, everyone believes that quitting always results in weight gain. In fact, only about a third of those who quit gain weight, and are more likely to be men, while another third stays the same, and the final third actually lose weight.

Nicotine gum proved effective, even more so when used as an adjunct to behavioral interventions, with a smoking cessation rate over 95 percent and abstinence rates of 60 percent after twelve months. This was, in fact, the best result anyone had achieved to date. The gum was appealing as a possible easy way out of addiction.

This gave me an important insight early on: people always seek the easiest solution to a problem, so a product that does not require much effort or understanding, that can be packaged, easily taken, and sold like a pill becomes a "magic bullet." Soon, the nicotine gum manufacturers who already knew this were marketing their new product, called "Nicorette".

As I watched the Nicorette gum marketing campaigns sweep the country, I wondered if behavioral researchers like myself could someday harness the power of the "magic bullet", applying it to behavioral prevention messages. We scientists rarely communicate our findings directly to the public, and when we do, it is in dry, technical language. The scientific community needed to start delivering more clear, concise, and persuasive messages the average person could understand. I filed that revelation away for future use.

The progress at work made me happy, but it couldn't match the sheer joy found in my personal life. I had met a wonderful man and fallen in love. Robert was tall, blue-eyed with curly brown hair, and of Irish descent. He had a dry sense of humor, which he used to great effect while regaling me with his stories. He came from a family of New York lawyers, but rather than going into law he chose to pursue an MBA. I could see a wild, adventurous side, too. He sang in a '50s rock and roll band, rode a motorcycle on the curvy coastal cliffs from Stinson Beach to San Francisco, and was a volunteer firefighter.

Robert lived in Stinson Beach but kept a ranch in Myers Flat with his business partner, and one weekend we drove up there. The scenic route meandered through verdant fields dotted with wineries and roadside farmer's markets. We passed through the towering redwood forest with trees wide enough to drive a car through. Yet none of these charming sights prepared me for the beauty of Robert's hilltop ranch. I stepped from the car, an orange VW bug, gawking at the panoramic view. The Pacific Ocean shimmered in the distance to the west. To the east, the frothy Eel River raged, and beyond I could see a sprawling Christmas tree farm flanked by scrub oak forests.

On the drive home from our magical weekend at the ranch, Robert asked me if I'd like to spend the summer there. I had no classes to worry about, so of course I said yes. That summer I passed the long, warm days riding horses, picking blackberries to bake into pies, and sipping wine as the sun set on the Pacific. In the fall, we spontaneously decided to go to Germany for the famous Bavarian Oktoberfest in Munich. Both of my brothers served in the U.S. Air Force, and at the time Jerry was stationed in Germany. He and his young family lived in Bad-Toelz near the snow-covered Bavarian Alps, so we stayed with them while enjoying the festivities.

Then, romantically, on Valentine's Day in 1979, Robert asked me to marry him and I said yes. We married that July, in a small church ceremony in northern Wisconsin surrounded by his family and mine. I was 26 years old.

Three years later, while finally getting close to finishing my doctoral dissertation, I became pregnant with my first child. I was so excited, but I knew I needed to complete the dissertation before giving birth, so the race was on. I became so obsessed with work that I wasn't fully present to enjoy my pregnancy and prepare myself for motherhood.

Finally, on August 12, 1982, after many revisions, I handed in my polished PhD dissertation on gender and psychosocial differences influencing smoking cessation. I was giddy with a sense of accomplishment and **RELIEF**! I remember the day so clearly, as it was unusually hot for San Francisco, which is memorable because San Francisco is typically cool even in summer. Mark Twain was known for saying, "The coldest winter I ever spent was a summer in San Francisco." But not today!! I laughed as I sweated from the unexpected heat and all the weight I had put on during the pregnancy. I was wearing a breezy maternity sundress with sandals. I basked in the sunlight for a few minutes, relishing my achievement, before heading home to collapse in sleep.

That very night I went into labor.

NAVIGATING CHANGE

"This can't be happening yet," I yelled at Robert as he timed my contractions. "I need more time to get used to being pregnant and to get ready for this!"

"It's happening," he said, doing a reasonable job of hiding his panic.

I labored through the night with Robert faithfully timing my contractions. By dawn, I knew it was time. Robert was starting to doze off, when in the loudest breathy voice I could muster I yelled, "Robert, I think the baby's coming. We need to go to the hospital, NOW!!" He jumped up and scrambled to put me and the bags into the car and off we rushed to the hospital. Fortunately, the San Francisco Kaiser Hospital was only a few minutes away from our apartment, and at 6 a.m. there was little traffic. So it wasn't long before I was being examined in the emergency room and heard the emergency room doctor yelling to his staff, "Everyone this baby is coming fast and its breech. We need to do an emergency C-section!" So in a matter of 45 minutes after arriving at the hospital, I was prepped and on the operating table having cesarean section surgery for the birth of my first child. It was all quite dramatic, and the result was nothing short of miraculous. As soon as she was delivered, they placed her near me so we could bond before general anesthesia to finish the surgery. When I came out of the anesthesia, they placed my beautiful baby girl in my arms. I was beyond elated. I was beaming. All I could do was smile from ear to ear and cry tears of joy.

NAVIGATING CHANGE

And that's how it happened that two of my life aspirations came true within hours of each other. My beautiful baby daughter, Marisa Ann, weighing seven pounds, two ounces, was born on Friday, August 13, 1982, just hours after I delivered my doctoral dissertation, which weighed in at just under five pounds.

NAVIGATING CHANGE

Robert & I at our wedding dinner at the Rib Mountain Ski Chalet in Wausau, WI, July 20th, 1979.

My doctoral graduation ceremony with my PhD in Health Psychology from UCSF, with my parents, San Francisco, CA, 1982.

NAVIGATING CHANGE

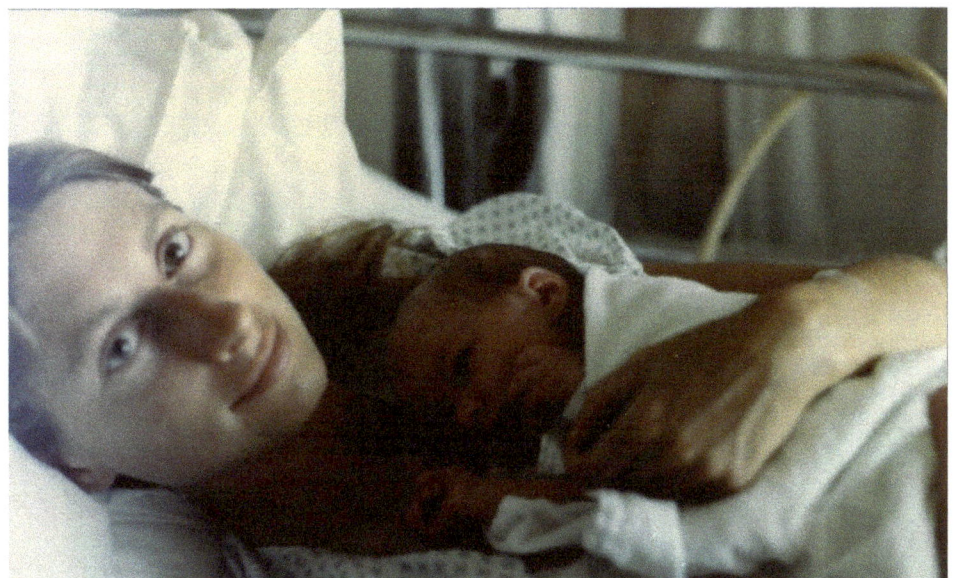

Me at San Francisco Kaiser Hospital, the birth of my first child, Marisa Ann, August 13th, 1982.

4

EMERGING CRISIS

The more you lose yourself in something bigger than yourself, the more energy you will have. - Norman Vincent Peale

I n June 1981, the CDC published an article in its Morbidity and Mortality Weekly Report about a rare lung infection in five young and previously healthy gay men in Los Angeles. The men had other unusual infections as well, indicating that their immune systems were compromised. Two of the five had already died by the time the report was published. The others died soon after. This article was the first official reporting of what later became known as GRID (Gay-Related Immune Deficiency) and would eventually be renamed AIDS.

Soon, similar reports were coming in from New York, Atlanta, and San Francisco. Journalists and television reporters picked up on the story. I can clearly remember watching a TV reporter for San Francisco's KRON talk nervously about what was happening in the city's

NAVIGATING CHANGE

Castro District, one of the first gay neighborhoods in the United States.

I had already known of the mysterious disease. My medical colleague at San Francisco General and UCSF, Paul Volberding, was reporting strange symptoms he was seeing in patients from the Castro. He recognized the chilling potential for a massive epidemic. The disease could leap into the heterosexual population through hemophiliacs, bisexuals, or perhaps via drug users who shared needles. At this point, we could not even rule out casual contact as a mode of transmission.

The dire public health threat required fast action, but the federal government seemed paralyzed by apathy. The conservative Reagan administration was loath to discuss—much less devote resources to—a disease of homosexuals. By default, the initial response fell to concerned doctors in San Francisco and other cities, who mobilized as best they could to get the word out to gay men, including by closing the bath houses.

I admired these courageous health professionals who eagerly jumped into the fray, and I knew my background and training could help in this terrifying new struggle. I joined an effort to learn more about the men who were coming into local hospitals with the telltale symptoms. My colleagues and I would administer questionnaires to these patients asking about their sexual history, trying to figure out the risk factors for infection.

NAVIGATING CHANGE

I'll admit it was a bit scary since we still didn't understand the disease's modes of transmission. I was careful as I collected the paper questionnaires they completed for me. Paper is porous, so it holds onto things. Previously, when working with smokers, I could smell tobacco on the questionnaires they had given me days earlier. Might I now be exposing myself to this deadly new disease simply by handling papers? I didn't know, but I set my concerns aside. The work was too important.

It was also far too exciting. Here I was, at the outset of my career, already fighting the spread of a mysterious pathogen. Most health professionals toiled their entire lives without such an historic opportunity. The gravity of my work invigorated me, and I frequently felt the incomparable rush of adrenaline, which kept me going despite little sleep.

Data collected during the interviews began to reveal some fascinating trends. The first thing that struck me was the sheer volume of sexual partners some people reported. The numbers ranged anywhere from fifteen partners to 150 to 1,000. I knew San Francisco had long been a sexually liberated environment for both gay and straight people, but some of the numbers defied belief. I soon realized that these interviewees included sex workers who engaged in multiple sexual encounters every day.

There were also men who reported having only a few partners, as well as some in monogamous relationships, yet had still become infected. On the surface this seemed perplexing, but it drove home a stark fact long known to epidemiologists: if you engage in unprotected sex, you're essentially having sex with not just your partner, but with every one of that person's previous partners. The bottom line was that we needed everyone to use condoms.

As a young person just starting out, I stayed on the lookout for a role model. This person would be someone in my field whose success I could try to emulate. Fortunately, I didn't need to look very far. As the epidemic ramped up, the CDC dispatched to San Francisco one of its top epidemiologists, Dr. Mary Guinan.

Guinan had begun her career developing new flavors of chewing gum because it was one of the few jobs available to a female chemist. Undeterred, she continued her education, earning a PhD in biochemistry and physiology from the University of Texas, and then an MD from Johns Hopkins. Her exploits as a "disease detective" would be featured in the National Geographic magazine, as well as a book and subsequent film called "And the Band Played On: People, Politics, and the AIDS Epidemic" by Randy Shilts. She later wrote a memoir entitled "Adventures of a Female Medical Detective: In Pursuit of Smallpox and AIDS", which I highly recommend.

Mary Guinan's success stemmed not only from her grit and determination, but from her sheer bravery. She worked closely with infected patients, sometimes risking an infection of her own. One such incident occurred shortly after she arrived in San Francisco. She was drawing blood from a large patient, an infected man big enough to play professional football, when suddenly he passed out and fell on top of her. As they tumbled to the floor, Guinan was stuck by his needle. Thankfully, the needle stick did not result in an infection, but she spent many months wondering and watching for symptoms.

Working on the front lines of an epidemic also carried hidden dangers that could not be anticipated. I experienced a scare early on, while in the comfort of my own home. It was evening, and I sat in the living room sorting a fresh batch of patient questionnaires while dinner cooked in the oven. Robert was reading the newspaper. My daughter Marisa, now about a year old, was playing at my feet. The oven timer went off, so I set down my papers on the coffee table and went to check on dinner.

When I returned from the kitchen, I froze in horror. My inquisitive toddler was playing with the questionnaires. As I came through the doorway, she was putting one of the papers in her mouth.

"Marisa, stop!" I shrieked, rushing over to her. My mind raced, trying to assess the danger. We still didn't know all the ways the disease could spread. I had accepted the fact I might be putting myself at risk, but of course my little girl was another matter entirely, and no amount of risk was acceptable. It never occurred to me she would be the least bit interested in the paper stack. I thought back to the smoking study, and how the smokers' questionnaires always smelled of tobacco.

"Do you think these papers could have traces of the infectious agent?" I worried out loud.

Robert shrugged. "Um, I don't know. I don't think so." The reply didn't comfort me very much. I looked down at Marisa's smiling little face and felt like crying. Robert returned to his newspaper. "Maybe just to be safe you should keep your questionnaires at the office from now on," he murmured. "Is dinner ready yet?"

I took Marisa to the bathroom and washed her hands and face, then I packed up the questionnaires and locked them in my briefcase. Robert's indifference annoyed me, but maybe he was right about leaving work materials at the office.

Today I know Marisa was never in any danger. HIV cannot spread via indirect contact. But in 1983 it certainly seemed plausible, and the terror I felt that night still stays with me.

The following year, on September 2, 1984, we would be blessed with the birth of our second daughter, Ilse Marie. This time I was fully present during the whole pregnancy and was well-prepared. I was really excited but also nervous because I was considered a "high risk pregnancy" due to having delivered my first child via cesarean section. I was determined this time to have a natural birthing experience if possible. I found a hospital in Berkeley that offered a compromise. I could have a home-like delivery in a natural, comforting setting, located adjacent to the hospital obstetrics surgery department, in case anything went wrong. This time I labored for twelve long hours in this setting and then delivered naturally, as planned.

It was an entirely different experience delivering naturally. Just as miraculous, more exhausting, and I could go home much sooner. I remember it being a gorgeous fall day as we drove home from the hospital with our precious little bundle of joy, feeling elated and relieved it had all gone well. It was now official. We had "graduated" from being a couple with a baby living in an apartment in the Haight-Ashbury district of the city, to being a full-fledged family living in a cozy three-bedroom home in the East Bay commuter suburb of Lafayette, with a barbecue and swing set in the backyard. Overnight, we woke up to a crazy busy new chapter; full-on family life had begun.

At work, I became a clinical assistant professor at UCSF. It was a temporary, part-time position, which suited me fine with two small children at home. Then, about a year later, San Diego State University (SDSU) offered me a full time academic appointment as assistant professor of health promotion in the Graduate School of Public Health. I was really excited about the offer as it was my first full-time academic appointment. Robert was supportive and felt I should take it. With his computer skills he could find work at SDSU. In the fall of 1985, we packed up our young family and moved south to the beachside community of Del Mar.

NAVIGATING CHANGE

I was 32 and academia suited me but also left me wanting more. I had been bitten by the public-health bug and craved the action of frontline work. AIDS had spiraled out of control, with more people being diagnosed in 1985 than in all previous years combined. Experts grimly predicted twice as many new cases in 1986. Yet I noticed in San Diego no one was talking about AIDS, and there was a big gap in prevention knowledge and research. I decided with my health psychology and health promotion research skills I had something to offer the community, the state, and beyond. Being from San Francisco, I had more early knowledge about AIDS than most people locally, and everyone was immediately coming to me for advice. I saw a need and an opportunity. People in San Diego didn't think they had a problem, but they did. I saw it firsthand and it was growing fast. I had to do something.

I decided I could blend my academic platform with a budding entrepreneurial spirit and launch a new center called the SDSU Center for Behavioral Research on HIV and STD. Thanks to serious networking with colleagues at SDSU and the local and state health departments, my first contract funds came in. I got a contract to evaluate the California Statewide HIV Anonymous Testing Site System, and with the funds I could pay myself, hire Robert, and more team members.

I learned that if you are able to scan your environment, identify gaps, and offer people what they need when they need it, they will find you and resources will follow. Even a young person early in their career could launch a new center or start-up and acquire the necessary leadership and management skills along the way. As Maya Angelou once said "Nothing succeeds like success. Get a little success and then just get a little more." We were off and running.

We were evaluating behavioral interventions that could slow the spread of AIDS, if people adopted them. The goal was to convince those at risk to get a HIV antibody test, protect themselves from transmission by wearing condoms correctly and consistently, and engage in honest discussions about past risks. Our efforts drew continued attention from the California Department of Public Health and eventually from the CDC, both of which awarded us contracts for further research.

My CDC contacts seemed particularly impressed, and I spoke with them on a regular basis. I didn't realize it at the time, but they were making plans for me.

Marisa (1) playing with her favorite toys at home in Lafayette, CA, 1983.

NAVIGATING CHANGE

Me (31) in Lafayette, CA pregnant with my second child, Ilse Marie, born Sept 2, 1984.

NAVIGATING CHANGE

Marisa (3) and Ilse (1) Lafayette, CA. 1985.

5

FAMILY TRANSITIONS

I am not afraid of storms, for I am learning how to sail my ship. - Louisa May Alcott

Like most professional women with small children, I soon felt pulled in multiple directions. The nonstop demands of work, keeping a home, paying bills, and seeing to the needs of two energetic little girls left me frazzled and stressed. I needed help. But money was really tight, like it is for everybody when you are young, just starting out with two kids, and sometimes only one spouse working. We even had a car repossessed at one point. It got better when Robert started working. "Being able to pay the bills" became a real motivator in my life, inspiring me throughout my early career to work really hard and always seek better paying positions as my family's expenses grew. As exhausting as my life had become, I loved every aspect of it, so I sacrificed and kept the family on a tight budget and kept exploring childcare options. Finally, we found a solution. We had some extra space in our rental house that could be turned into a bedroom. So we looked for someone who could provide part-time childcare in exchange for room and board and a modest stipend. We found a charming French woman named Marie who had moved from France to Del Mar. She was an au pair, a pair of helping hands, and she made all the difference.

Marie helped me with the girls before and after the limited daycare provided by the university (they offered a subsidized daycare center for students and staff right next to my office), some weekends and special events, and taught the girls to be polite and respect their elders, to speak French (they picked it up so easily, including the French accent), and of course to love a good croissant. She became a part of our family. My days were still filled, but with Marie's help I no longer struggled to get everything done. In July 1986, we gave her a month off, Robert took some time for himself, and I planned a two-week trip with the girls to Wisconsin to visit with my family.

My parents adored the girls, and the girls absolutely loved spending time in Wisconsin at Grandma and Grandpa's house and the cottage (just like I had as a kid), baking cookies with Grandma, riding on Grandpa's small tractor, and playing with their cousins, my sister's kids. While we were there they begged me to stay longer with Grandma and Grandpa, but I had to return to San Diego. So I decided to let them stay. I planned to return to get them in a week. Everyone was happy.

NAVIGATING CHANGE

Dad drove me to the airport, like he had done so many times before, but this time seemed different. He was unusually quiet. When it was time to board my plane, I noticed a tear in his eye.

"Goodbye, honey," he said, hugging me tightly. "Love you." "I love you too, Dad. Take care of my little angels for me." We were standing in his old airport. It was the place where he had taken me up in the little Cessna years earlier, letting me experience the thrill of flying. Before boarding, I turned and waved. He waved back but looked terribly sad. I didn't think much of it. Dad could get emotional at times.

The plane carried me back to San Diego, where the house felt so quiet and empty without the girls.

A day after I was back and had just finished unpacking, the phone rang. It was my brother calling from Wisconsin, and immediately I knew something was wrong.

"Debbie, you had better come back. Dad just had a heart attack. They took him to the hospital."

I was back on an airplane four hours later. It was the longest flight of my life, with each minute lasting an hour. Tears blurred my vision as I struggled to hold back my sobs. I needed to see Dad, to tell him again how much I loved him.

It was too late. Dad died before I got there. He was just 55 years old.

Back at the house, Mom seemed to be holding up fairly well. But then just as soon as the last neighbor left, she turned to me and collapsed in my arms sobbing. "He loved me his whole life, 'til the day he died!" Gasping, she cried, "What am I gonna do now?" I guided her to the sofa and sat her down, hugging her and holding her tightly. As soon as she could breathe again, she tried to recount what had happened.

"I just went to pick up some birthday cards at the drugstore. I wasn't gone for more than 25 minutes," she began. "When I got home, I walked into the living room and there he was," she gasped for air again and cried, "laying on the floor with little Marisa and Ilse standing over him, urging him to wake up. They were whimpering and saying "Grandpa, the game is over, you can get up now!" My mom was in shock, and so was I.

Marisa was four years old and Ilse just two. I couldn't imagine what must have been going through their little minds. A good neighbor had volunteered to watch them while I helped Mom regain her composure that day and deal with the details. When I brought the girls home and comforted them, they didn't want to talk. So I just held them, ever so tightly, flooded by my own emotions and fighting back tears. Like any good mother, I didn't want them to see how upset I really was.

I worried they might have post-traumatic-experience symptoms, so I talked it over with a child psychologist. She felt any long-term damage was unlikely because they were so young, especially Ilse, and she said we had done well to assure the girls it wasn't their fault. Still, I worried, particularly about Marisa since she was older, but thankfully no symptoms ever appeared. In fact, a few years later Marisa wrote a school essay about the most important day in her life. She wrote about being with her grandfather the day he died. Her words were so poignant and beautiful that I knew she had fully processed the experience, as well as a child can.

As for me, I couldn't stop thinking of Dad's apparent sadness at the airport the last time I saw him alive. Did he sense he was going to die? I still wonder about that to this day.

As for Mom, she eventually recovered, and would remarry. As it turned out, she married my high school friend's dad, Jim, who was also a friend of my Dad and had lost his wife around the same time we lost Dad. Linda and I were friends and homecoming queen candidates together in high school, and now we would be step-sisters too. Seemingly overnight, I now had a large, blended family to adjust to with my three married siblings and their kids, a new step-dad, four new married step-siblings and their kids, and my own family of four.

Ilse (2) and me (33) at our family's cottage in Chetek, WI, right before Dad died in 1986.

NAVIGATING CHANGE

Ilse, me and Marisa in Tiverton, RI. during the summer of 1994.

6

CULTURE SHOCK

You may not control all the events that happen to you, but you can decide not to be reduced by them. - Maya Angelou

With time, I came to terms with Dad's death and life slowly returned to normal. I was 34 years old, happy at work, and content living in Del Mar, California. I didn't foresee any major changes in my life, which typically means one is about to arrive. In this instance, change came in the form of a job offer from CDC. In July 1987, they invited me to become the first psychologist in history to join their world-renowned Epidemic Intelligence Service (EIS). The position was located at CDC headquarters in Atlanta, Georgia.

A cross-country move would have been no problem when I was single, but I had a family now. If I accepted, I'd need to find new schools for the girls and support my husband while he looked for a new job. CDC sweetened the deal by offering Robert work in expanding their epidemiology software program called Epi Info. This turned out to be a great move for Robert. He and his team would turn CDC's Epi Info into a premier disease surveillance software program, earning him national recognition, the chance to lead disease surveillance at the 1996 Olympics, and travel widely internationally. So it was settled; we were moving to Atlanta. Even our au pair Marie agreed to make the move.

As soon as we set foot in Georgia, I sensed an enormous cultural difference. The Old South mentality still prevailed, especially regarding female professionals. The first shock came when I went shopping for work clothes. All I needed was standard business attire but finding an outfit without ruffles and frills proved nearly impossible. Worse, no social infrastructure existed for young mothers with careers. I couldn't find any preschools with full-time care, only Mother's Day Out programs that gave moms one day a week to go shopping. Fortunately, CDC solved this problem when it opened an excellent daycare facility on its premises shortly after I arrived.

At work, I still couldn't believe the honor I had received. For a health psychologist, being recruited into the EIS was like a jazz musician being recruited into the London Symphony Orchestra. Each year, just 45–50 new officers were indoctrinated into the two-year epidemiology training program. Nearly all were medical doctors. As a health psychologist—and a woman—I most definitely stood out as different, but I wasn't going to let that stop me or reduce me in any way. They had recruited me, but they weren't quite sure what to make of me yet.

The training was fascinating. We learned how to track population-based health threats. We also came to understand the principles of attributable risk, and how to identify causative agents. Essentially, we were learning what to do if, for example, there was an outbreak of an infectious agent or food poisoning at a fast-food restaurant or aboard a cruise ship. You had to figure out what was contaminated, then isolate and treat the victims, and control further spread of the outbreak. At least that was the process in its simplest form. As we would soon find out, it became much more complicated with a pathogen like HIV.

The training program ended, and I passed all the tests and administrative hurdles, becoming a freshly minted epidemiologist in 1989 in the Division of HIV/STD Prevention. It was a great place to work, but I quickly ran into a problem.

CDC was full of smart, altruistic people. In their youth they had been conscientious objectors and Peace Corps volunteers, idealists who, like me, wanted to make the world a better place. I loved working in that environment, but frankly I did not fit in at first. My colleagues were mostly male, older physicians, full of ego and very experienced in treating disease and conducting disease surveillance, but not in behaviorally preventing it. My youthful fresh perspectives and behavioral science paradigms were new to them. In meetings, my comments would often be dismissed with polite head nods or simply ignored altogether. The more I spoke up, the more I felt like I alienated them, so instead I went silent, observed the group dynamics, and learned to read the room. As with any group, there were leaders who commanded everyone's attention and respect. When these individuals spoke, the rest listened. That's when I had an epiphany: the source of a message matters just as much as its content, and in a group setting, the source matters even more.

It's simple when you think about it. Picture an outsider who suddenly stands up and announces, "I have the answer to this problem and here's what we should do." That person, even after making a convincing argument, likely will be dismissed simply because they lack standing. I know it works that way because it happened to me many times during those early years at CDC. I had the right message, but I was not the right person to deliver it.

My solution was to find an ally, someone who everyone trusted and respected. I would identify a thoughtful, influential member of the group, and then arrange a one on-one meeting where I could make my case. Once I won that leader over, the hardest part of my task was done. I could sit back and watch the leader persuade the rest of the group. I called this technique "leading from behind the scenes" and it worked.

NAVIGATING CHANGE

The fact that I didn't receive credit for the idea was fine with me. I knew I was contributing to the greater good, which mattered most. Besides, with time, people began to realize the true source of the ideas, and once that happened, I gained enough standing to present them myself. I no longer had to lead from behind the scenes because people knew I had good ideas. In other words, they now saw me as a leader.

During this period, I had the good fortune of working for Dr. Jim Curran, the executive director of CDC's Office of HIV/AIDS, the public face of AIDS, and a great public health leader. He would later become the dean of Emory University's School of Public Health, where I also worked as an adjunct professor. Jim always had a way of saying the most encouraging things at exactly the right moment. He came up with some of the most inspiring and insightful phrases; they would stick with me my whole career. In the early days of AIDS, when we were conducting epidemiological research on those who had become infected with HIV, he always reminded us about human dignity.

"Remember the faces," he would say. "Behind every statistic is a person, and each person has a story. Take the time to listen and really hear them." I later learned that Jim had gotten this sound advice himself from his adviser, the world famous leader of smallpox eradication and global health, Bill Foege. And it's likely Bill got it from his adviser. There was and still is an amazingly strong sense of public health history, legacy, and succession at CDC. Many top directors had their start as CDC EIS officers.

Despite this context and his hectic schedule, Jim always made time for me. He loved to hear my contrary perspectives, and he was only disappointed if I didn't have an opinion. I was fortunate to have two such incredible bosses at CDC; the other was Dr. Eugene McCray, director of CDC's Global AIDS Program (GAP), a pioneering medical epidemiologist and global leader in TB and HIV. He really embraced evaluation and nurtured the path I was going down, focusing my energy on bringing better monitoring and evaluation to the Global AIDS Program. As I would later discover, outstanding leaders are hard to come by, and a self-centered or incompetent leader can completely ruin an otherwise perfect job. Knowing when to walk away is also a skill that I would develop over time.

You don't have to settle for a bad boss. When you interview for a new position, evaluate your potential supervisor just as closely as they are evaluating you. Your boss can mean all the difference between workplace happiness or misery, success or failure, so be on the lookout for red flags. If your instincts say you'll have trouble working for that person, then you probably will, so it's best to look elsewhere.

I now had a rewarding job with an exceptional boss. I had gained the attention of my evaluation colleagues in the American Evaluation Association, who in 1997 awarded me with the prestigious Alva & Gunnar Myrdal Award for exceptional Leadership in Government Service. I had earned the respect of old-school male physicians who previously wouldn't give me the time of day. This achievement really hit home the day CDC director, Dr. David Satcher, held a special briefing to acknowledge my efforts and gave me an award for "Leadership in Advancing the Behavioral and Social Sciences at CDC." As the leading EIS-trained health psychologist, I could finally make a real impact evaluating America's response to AIDS.

So far that response had been weak and ineffectual, and I intended to find out why.

Me receiving award for Advancing Behavioral & Social Science at CDC from Dr. David Satcher, CDC Director, Atlanta, 1996.

NAVIGATING CHANGE

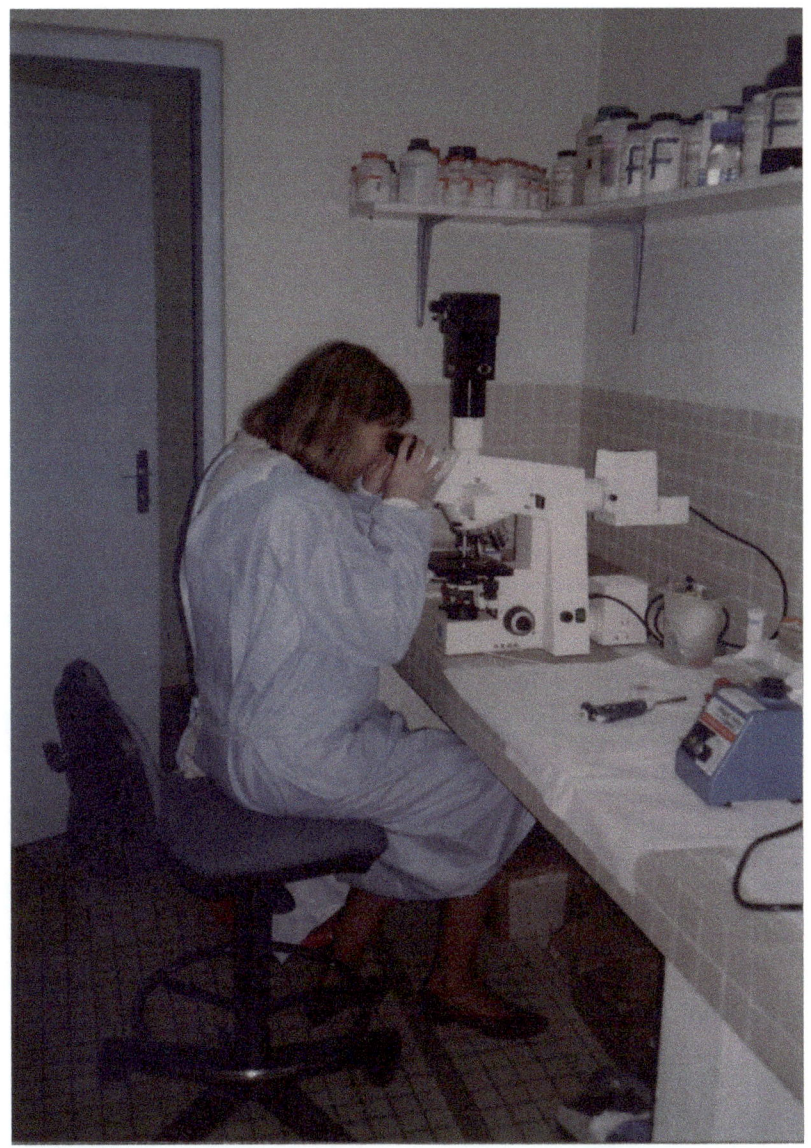

Me looking at HIV for the first time in the new CDC HIV Projet RETRO-CI lab in Abidjan, Ivory Coast, West Africa, 1996.

NAVIGATING CHANGE

1996 CDC Scientific Advisory Team, Projet RETRO-CI, Ivory Coast (l-r) Drs. Helene Gayle, Rene Ekpini, David Satcher & me.

STRENGTHENING, MONITORING AND EVALUATION OF NATIONAL AIDS PROGRAMS IN THE CONTEXT OF THE EXPANDED RESPONSE, APRIL 23-26, 2001 ENTEBBE - UGANDA

CDC Global AIDS Program Director Eugene McCray & team establishing the Global AIDS Program office in Zambia, late 2001.

NAVIGATING CHANGE

A flat tire draws curious children on the road from Siem Reap to the CDC office in Phnom Penh, Cambodia, 2003.

7

ADVERSARIES TO ALLIES

I am a very strong believer in listening and learning from others. - Ruth Bader Ginsburg

The most frustrating part of fighting AIDS in the 1980s was the feeling that we had both arms tied behind our backs. We had identified the steps that would work, but because of politics we couldn't get them implemented. Our recommendations included: teaching safe sex in schools, promoting condom use, and doing outreach with sex workers and with drug users about the importance of clean needles. These interventions, unfortunately, were political lightning rods. No elected official wanted to get near them. Part of the problem was CDC's reputation in Washington as a maverick agency, which it had earned long before AIDS arrived. Back then, a headquarters in Atlanta made sense, but over the decades it led to distrust from Washington power brokers, who felt they could not keep the agency under heel from 600 miles away. The fact that CDC hired a lot of former conscientious objectors and Peace

Corps volunteers didn't help its reputation with conservative politicians. I knew of the tension but felt there had to be some way of building alliances in Washington, so I set off for the nation's capital on a fact-finding mission. The trip's most insightful moment came at the National Press Club, after I watched reporters grill a sincere U.S. congressman over the lack of a comprehensive national AIDS policy. As the interrogation ended and the reporters filed away, I approached him. His forehead glistened with sweat.

"Excuse me, sir, I'm a CDC epidemiologist. Do you have one more minute for a question I've been struggling with?" He seemed intrigued, or at least grateful I was not a reporter. "Sure, fire away."

I took a deep breath. This was an important opportunity to make a difference, and I wanted to get it right. "We know how to slow the spread of HIV. My colleagues and I have been sharing the evidence, and it's the strongest evidence I have ever seen. But we still aren't seeing a national policy to match the science. In fact, the reverse seems increasingly true."

He smiled. It was a politician's smile, but I sensed he genuinely wanted to help.

"What can we do differently?" I asked. "Any suggestions?" He started to speak, then hesitated. "This is off the record, right?"

I nodded.

"First, you scientists need to simplify your message. Don't just send us a long, technical evaluation report. Repackage it into a simple, easy-to-read policy brief. Second, don't bother us with findings that split hairs or have limited impact. We need clear, compelling information to get people's attention. Tell us about the big findings that affect large numbers of people and produce significant results."

As I listened, I knew he was right. I'd sat in too many jargon-filled meetings myself that became bogged down in minutiae.

"This last one is really important," he continued. "You need to be timely. Don't give us results right after we've finished legislating on a topic. We won't be able to use them until the next cycle, if at all."

"I understand," I assured him.

He sighed. "Truth be told, if your findings go against the prevailing values and attitudes of the people in my district, and my party, then it's going to be very difficult for me to act on the information."

An aide interrupted, saying it was time to go. I thanked him profusely and watched the staffers hurry him off to his next meeting. Then I packed up my briefcase and headed for the airport. I couldn't wait to return to Atlanta and share my newfound political insight.

Back at CDC, no one seemed to care. I should have known. They were buried too deeply in their various projects to bother learning Washington gamesmanship. Their passion was science, political realities were a frustrating annoyance. It was a fact driven home every time my AIDS colleagues and

NAVIGATING CHANGE

I went out to a restaurant together. The dinner conversation always morphed into a loud debate about whatever we were working on at the time.

"Do you think men will ever consistently use condoms?" someone would ask the table. "What makes a man decide to use a condom or not?"

Once the questions got started, they kept coming in rapid-fire succession. Each response grew louder than the last as the participants jockeyed to be heard.

"What facilitates the different infection rates in men versus women?"

"How much sex, and with what type of partners, are people in different countries having?"

Finally, our server would come over and ask us to hold it down. Everyone would stop and shyly look around at the people staring from nearby tables. But inevitably this self-consciousness faded, and the loud questions resumed.

"What kind of sex—vaginal, anal, or oral—do you think transmits the virus the most efficiently?"

Eventually I became mindful of our bad habit and would remind the group. "Hey, guys, we are getting a bit loud again. Remember, not everyone works with this stuff and feels as passionately about it as we do."

I couldn't fault them. These were world-class disease detectives trying to solve the mystery of AIDS. They really didn't know they were disturbing other people. At the end of the meal, we always apologized to our neighbors and left a big tip.

A virus loves nothing more than when humans stick their heads in the sand, and society's inability to discuss sexual issues back in those days created so much unnecessary harm. I always considered my mother a typical American, so I would use her as a barometer of the average citizen's views on AIDS. At times it could be a real eye-opener.

"Debbie, what exactly do you do at the CDC?" Mom once asked during a visit home.

It was the sort of question I dreaded. Explaining the AIDS epidemiologic research and sexually transmitted disease (STD, also called STI, sexually transmitted infections) contact tracing I was doing would be difficult, so I decided to keep it simple. "I'm studying the fear and stigma that makes people so reluctant to talk about AIDS."

She nodded supportively, so I continued. "There are so many myths and misperceptions. People seem to think it'll just go away if they just don't talk about it, but that only fuels any epidemic!"

Mom smiled. "Oh, honey, I'm so glad you moved on from working on, you know," and her voice dropped to a whisper, "from working on VD."

I was stunned. Venereal Disease (VD) was her generation's term for STDs. She had interpreted my reply in a way I couldn't even begin to fathom.

NAVIGATING CHANGE

Mom leaned back in her chair, visibly relieved. "Now I know what to say when my bridge club asks, 'So what's Debbie doing these days?'"

After that, Mom and I stuck to superficial conversations about my work. She only wanted to hear about the places I traveled and the safety of the countries I visited. In retrospect, I guess Mom truly was a typical American of the time. Sexual intercourse, STDs, and especially gay sex were taboo topics, not to be discussed in polite company. Add to that Washington's reluctance to develop a science-based national policy, and it was the perfect storm for HIV.

The only people seeking frank discussions about AIDS were the gay activists. The most organized and effective group was ACT UP (AIDS Coalition To Unleash Power), which had formed in New York City and was led by the prominent gay activist and writer Larry Kramer. As a direct-action group, ACT UP wanted media attention. They wanted to be arrested. Their favorite tactic was in-your-face booing and noise making at large public meetings.

I first saw ACT UP in 1987, at the Second International AIDS Conference in Washington, D.C. The activists booed and shouted, delaying the conference's opening address by none other than President Ronald Reagan. Ten thousand people had gathered to hear what the president would say. I was sitting in the front row, just off to the left of the stage, and I could see Reagan and his aides fidgeting behind the curtain as they waited for the booing to subside.

The president obviously didn't realize his lapel microphone was already live. I saw him turn to an aide and say with disgust, "Can you believe this? It must be a completely gay crowd."

His insensitive comment echoed across the auditorium, sending the activists into a frenzy. They didn't calm down for almost two hours, and by then the entire opening session had been derailed.

Gay activists viewed CDC as just another federal agency, a deceitful puppet of Reagan and his cronies. As a result, two natural allies against AIDS wasted precious time as adversaries. The conflict came to a head in January 1990. Hundreds of activists rioted at the Georgia State Capitol in protest of the state's sodomy laws. Afterwards, they made their way to the main CDC campus on Clifton Road. I didn't work in the Clifton campus at the time, I worked in another one of CDC's seven locations, but I had a meeting there that day and became trapped.

Someone managed to hoist a lavender flag up the campus flagpole. A few protestors tried to break into the building, but then police in full riot gear moved in. With helmets covering their faces and batons raised, they lined up shoulder-to-shoulder and pushed the crowd back. In the end, more than 50 people were handcuffed and hauled away in police vans.

After that, the stormy relationship between CDC and the activist groups gradually began to evolve. "We need each other too much to be enemies," Dr. Jim Curran advised both sides at a small strategy session after the protests. "We need to learn how to dance seamlessly with each other in our mutual cause." We promised to share our scientific findings quickly and directly with them, so they could better educate members of the gay community about the latest findings and continued importance of practicing safer sex.

Our dance, as Jim put it, certainly had its missteps. Another riot occurred at the end of 1990, when protestors broke into the CDC satellite office where I worked, terrorizing the staff, chanting "Where's Mary Guinan? CDC is killing women." They were angry with CDC for not updating the AIDS case definition to include conditions unique to women, and Mary was lead on this aspect. They chanted and laid on the floor until police officers came and carried them out one by one. It would take time to convince the activist groups that we were not the enemy, but eventually it happened. Ultimately, ACT UP and its partners would become highly vocal CDC advocates in Washington, using the CDC information to lobby the politicians to send more AIDS-targeted funding our way.

8

PANDEMIC SCIENCE, MYTHS AND HEROES

Be a good ancestor. Stand for something bigger than yourself. Add value to the earth during your sojourn.
- Marion Wright Edelman

The virus didn't care one bit about politics or social norms. Nor did it care about the sexual orientation, gender, or age of the people it infected. International boundaries meant nothing to it, and HIV quickly spread to every nation on earth. One of the global scientists examining how the virus really thrived whenever science, myths, and politics collided was Dr. Peter Piot, one of the world's foremost AIDS heroes and former executive director of the Joint United Nations Programme on AIDS (UNAIDS). He aptly observed in his 2015 memoir "AIDS: Between Science and Politics" that, "Science without politics has no impact, politics without science can be dangerous, and without programs people don't benefit." I would later work for Peter at UNAIDS in Geneva. As I watched him, I learned firsthand how to juggle the competing forces at the nexus of public health science, myths, and politics.

As the HIV/AIDS pandemic spread, the value-laden politics of sex continued to inflict deadly consequences, especially on gay men. My colleagues and I wanted to better understand the risk factors for these men and help design more effective programs. We needed to help them be safer, so we started researching sexual behavior interventions with gay men. During this time, I learned a lot about human sexuality, the intimacy needs between men, and the differences and similarities between homosexuality and heterosexuality around the world.

At CDC, we came to use the phrase "men who have sex with men" in our prevention messages. It enabled men who didn't self-identify as gay to also consider the interventions we were developing as relevant for them too. This simple wording change was an important step forward, but we still struggled to get our message out to the public so they could take the appropriate precautions. We were handicapped by the political environment of the times.

I took part in a door-to-door campaign in local Atlanta communities. I'd knock on a door and introduce myself, then hand the person a brochure and say something like, "If you think you or anyone you know may be at risk, you can get tested. Here are local clinics where you can go for a test. Any questions?" In my experience, nobody ever had any questions.

NAVIGATING CHANGE

Next, we tried sending contact tracers into Atlanta gay bars with brochures that encouraged men to come in for testing. It was a disaster. Nobody wanted to be seen taking a brochure or even talking to a CDC epidemiologist, for fear others would assume they were sick and avoid them. We realized that many men avoided getting tested because they were afraid of the results. Some harbored suspicions that the testing wouldn't be totally anonymous. In fact, many of our early outreach attempts for gay men were so misguided that we were actually "driving HIV underground."

The turning point came when we started targeting specific audiences with a message tailored just for them. We abandoned the vague public service announcements (known as PSAs) that were suitable for all audiences, but effective for none. To make an impact, we needed precise targeting of custom messages that we would get from the audience members themselves. For example, in Seattle, after interviewing men who have sex with men we found that many men reported they would use condoms if it was perceived as acceptable and the norm. We also found that 75% of a small group of men sampled reported using condoms. So we piloted a communication campaign based on the message: "THREE OUT OF FOUR GAY MEN IN SEATTLE ARE USING CONDOMS . . . ARE YOU ONE OF THEM? DON'T BE LEFT OUT!" and it worked. Condom use in Seattle sky-rocketed.

NAVIGATING CHANGE

My evaluation work routinely took me to the Caribbean because the epidemic was raging there. I felt I was making a difference, and the trips to Puerto Rico, the place of my birth, felt particularly meaningful. I would go into a country and evaluate their efforts to curb the disease with condoms, education, HIV counseling, and testing. I did the same in Asia and Africa, and with time my travels gave me special insights into the wide variety of national AIDS responses.

On the depressing side was Botswana, the home of my friend Eleanora, who tragically died of AIDS in her early twenties. Many Botswanans refused to believe there was a crisis, even when they saw people dying all around them. You would hear explanations, from public officials and private citizens alike, that the deaths had other causes. Sometimes, when faced with perplexing danger, human nature compels us to deny that there really is a threat. We go about our daily lives in denial hoping the problem will simply resolve itself.

Embedded in Botswana culture was a strong suspicion of foreigners, which only fed the denial. Health officials routinely told me things like: "It's not as bad as the World Health Organization statistics show. Rich and powerful countries are just trying to scare us. We know how to take care of our people and we'll do this our own way. We just don't trust outsiders." Eventually, Botswana did accept outside help, but by then almost a third of the country was infected.

Every AIDS-plagued nation I visited had one common feature—the courage and tenacity of its frontline healthcare workers. Hospital workers in developing countries are not paid very well, so they often work multiple jobs, walking many miles because of a lack of transportation. Despite these circumstances, they remain utterly dedicated to their patients. For the rest of my career, I would always remember the pandemic's frontline workers and focus on easing their burden.

In Uganda, the nurses knew what was happening in their communities as much as, if not more than, the doctors. They understood the disease's transmission dynamics and what needed to be done to stop it. These nurses worked with scant resources and little thanks or respect, yet they never gave up. They never gave up. They devised some of the most brilliant care solutions for their patients and politely listened to the well-paid experts who showed up from abroad, supposedly with all the answers.

Once, in a high-level meeting, I saw a brave Ugandan nurse break protocol by speaking up. This petite woman, who cared so deeply for her patients, clearly had heard enough. She stood up, dressed in her crisp, clean white uniform, and spoke eloquently about why the people of her community were getting infected and what could be done to prevent further transmission. The all-male healthcare team sat there stunned by her audacity, but they couldn't deny the wisdom of her words.

I respected these women and their quiet dignity immensely. Watching them work always tugged at my heartstrings. I was in awe of the human spirit's desire, against all odds, to survive, and the brilliance and light that would come from the least expected places and from the least powerful of people.

NAVIGATING CHANGE

HIV Counseling & Testing Site offering free condoms; Marisa (in window's reflection) & me, Soweto, South Africa, 1999.

South African HIV peer educators at the Mandela Health Clinic in Soweto, Johannesburg, South Africa, 1999.

Me & Ties Boerma, Director, Measure Evaluation, UNC, discussing AIDS indicators for West Africa, Dakar, Senegal, 2003.

CDC Strategic Information and Monitoring & Evaluation Field Officers first global meeting in Atlanta, GA, 2004.

Me training Jemma University faculty to be HIV M&E trainers, Adama (near Addis Ababa), Ethiopia, January, 2005.

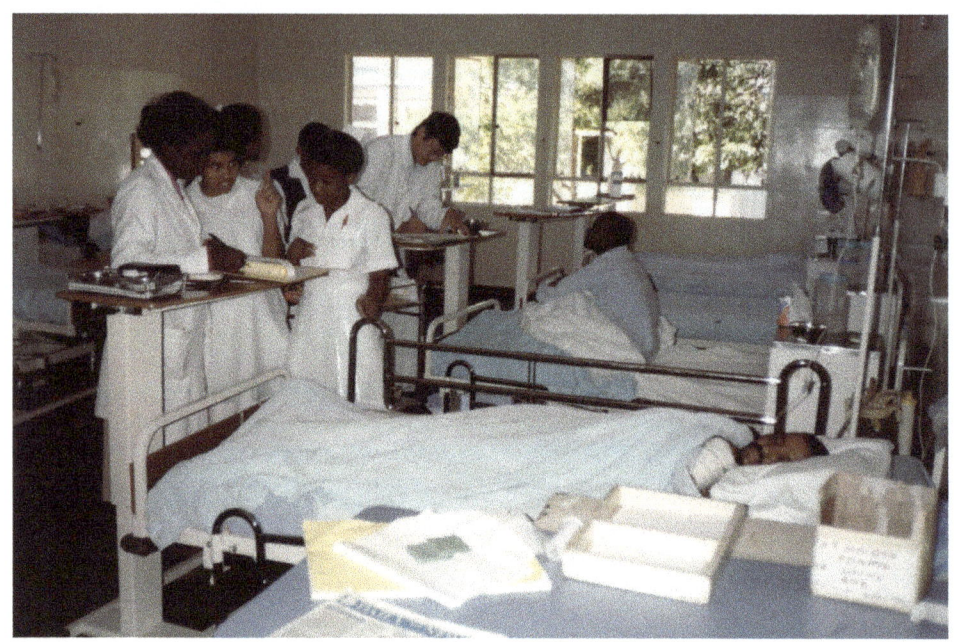

Nurses at AIDS hospital in Kampala, Uganda, 1999.

9

SPRINGBOARD FROM SETBACKS

Although the world is full of suffering, it is also full of overcoming it. - Helen Keller

My travels took me to remote corners of the planet and exposed me to the full spectrum of human behavior. I learned that attitudes toward sex varied widely by culture. Back in Wisconsin, sex was the most private of matters, but in parts of Asia and the Caribbean, sex was merely a service to be bought and sold. Thailand has long been known for its international sex trade, making it a global target for effective HIV prevention. Yet even I was unprepared for what I found there. Once, I was visiting a CDC officer stationed in Chang Rai, and he said, "Let's take a drive. I want to show you something." We drove for a while, eventually passing a colorful billboard with familiar cartoon characters. Then we reached a gate, where an attendant waved us through. The dirt road led us to rows of tiny huts. Painted on the door of each hut was Snow White or Cinderella or Sleeping Beauty, and inside was a young girl dressed as the character on the door. I was standing in a Disney-inspired sex theme park. It sickened me. Many of these girls were sex-trafficking victims. They had been kidnapped from other countries and forced to work in places like this. But not all arrived that way. Some girls had been sent here by their parents to earn money for the family.

These girls had no rights, no control over the sale of their own bodies. They were sex slaves, and HIV infection was probably the last thing on their long list of worries. But in fact, it needed to be first, because AIDS was killing them. I wanted to shut this place down and those like it, but that was impossible. We couldn't change engrained cultural values about sex, but at least we could take steps to keep these people alive.

In the sex trade, many men will pay extra for sex without a condom. This of course can be tempting to greedy brothel owners. However, those same brothel owners realize they need disease-free workers if they wish to remain profitable. That simple fact became the key to widespread condom use in Thailand's sex industry. The government developed the aggressive "National 100% Condom Use Campaign," which we evaluated and found to be quite effective. Condom use dramatically increased between sex workers and clients, especially in the brothels.

Thai programs to prevent sex trafficking of young girls and boys and provide rescue orphanages also sprung up. I visited several such orphanages. I was always amazed at how, even though these children had experienced so much trauma and suffering in their young lives, once taken out of those settings, and shown kindness, love, and education, how resilient they were as they overcame their past. Once again my heart was warmed by the powerful resilience of the human spirit.

Government support for HIV prevention was starting to take shape back at home, too. We had accepted that no useful national AIDS policy would be coming out of Washington, and instead sought help at the state and local levels. For example, Congresswoman Nancy Pelosi from San Francisco used our evidence to help California implement more rational HIV adolescent prevention policies. It illustrated an important lesson for anyone seeking change. Find people who are willing to listen and make them your allies. Don't waste time on people who are determined to shut you out.

Fortunately, the 1990s brought to Washington an increasing number of sympathetic ears. Led by President Bill Clinton, this new regime made the fight against AIDS a priority, and we finally received the prevention funding that would make a difference. Clinton's Leadership and Investment for Fighting an Epidemic (LIFE) initiative garnered congressional support for $5 billion dollars in global HIV funding. It was an exciting time to be out on the front lines, helping to put those resources to good use.

At home in Atlanta, the situation was far less encouraging. Robert and I had grown emotionally distant. We both traveled for work, with Robert traveling increasingly often. I came to think of myself as a "married single parent." Robert seldom seemed to be around or available to help when I needed him. And when we were together, it seemed all we did was argue. I tried everything I could think of and kept telling myself things would improve, but in reality they were slowly getting worse. To cope, I focused on taking care of the girls. Watching them grow brought me immense joy and sustained me during those years. I also focused on work and tried to keep a work-life balance. But I got lost in the shuffle; there was no time for me. All I could manage was listening to my favorite music to lift my spirits as I sang along doing household chores or driving the girls to and from school. Years later, it's fun to see my daughter sing along to the same songs, and to the ones she's added, as she drives her own sons to school.

At CDC, a position for which I was uniquely qualified opened up—a job I badly wanted. My education and practical experience perfectly matched the job requirements. The interviews went smoothly, with the hiring committee showing great interest in my presentations. According to the office rumor mill, I was a clear favorite.

The rumors were wrong. A last-minute candidate, a man who had spent his entire career in academia, flew in and wowed the all-male hiring committee. They chose him immediately. I felt betrayed and crushed. Colleagues took me aside and told me they were appalled by the decision. This man lacked the necessary field experience, and everyone knew it. The setback made me numb, pushing me into a sort of professional disengagement. I still did the necessary work but took no pleasure in it. Ultimately, the academic failed at his job and had to be fired, but that unfortunate outcome gave me no comfort.

When I look back now, I realize being passed over for that job was probably the best thing that could have happened at that point in my life. In a strange way, the universe may have been watching out for me. The distraction of a new job, with all its responsibilities, probably would have kept me from focusing on my personal life, failing marriage, and taking what would be a first devastatingly painful step toward divorce.

Divorce at its core is an identity crisis. Some may consider divorce a failure, but it is NOT a failure if what is ending is a dysfunctional relationship, with the goal of a healthier future for all. I needed to disentangle myself from the "we" identity I had lived for the past twenty years and re-establish an "I" identity. It was going to take time. Then there were the painful custody negotiations yet to come. I tried to shelter the girls, who were fourteen and sixteen, from these negotiations, but they were old enough to have a say. I was trying hard to make a better life for them, for everyone. In the end, we worked out a shared custody arrangement. In November 1998 we finally divorced. I was 45. Slowly, we adapted to this new life. It was not easy, on any level, and

NAVIGATING CHANGE

to this day I feel it was the hardest emotional thing I have ever done. Since paying all the bills on a single income was rough, at work I took on more responsibilities hoping to get promoted. We were making solid progress in the fight against AIDS. Finally, I was promoted. I became the first associate director for monitoring and evaluation in CDC's Global AIDS Program. But it was a job that required me to travel the world at breakneck speed, rapidly setting up new field offices. When traveling, I wasn't always sure what time zone I was in, so I kept it simple—I just told myself, "If it is daylight, stay awake. If it is dark, sleep."

In 2001, President George W. Bush took office. I didn't realize it at the time, but this political event would have far-reaching consequences for scientists like myself. The new administration wanted to revamp and rename the government's AIDS response, and my colleagues and I got dragged into the administrative task of coming up with a new name. For two years, we wasted precious time arguing with other agencies about a title. There were endless debates over simple words. For example, we couldn't use "research" because Congress had insisted the new funding was for action and not research. Finally, the White House approved PEPFAR, which stood for President's Emergency Plan for AIDS Relief. (I guess a perfect acronym like LIFE only comes along once in a lifetime.)

The naming debacle was just the start. In 2002, the Bush administration used some of my CDC colleagues as tools for political revenge. It all started at the XIV International AIDS Conference in Barcelona, Spain, where Bush's director of health and human services, Tommy Thompson, was giving a speech. At this conference, like many others, AIDS protesters had shown up to voice their displeasure with administration policy. When Thompson took the stage to deliver his speech, they booed incessantly. Of course, I had witnessed many such protests in the past and thought little of it.

Shortly after we returned to our offices in Atlanta, some of my CDC colleagues received an unofficial request from Washington. My colleagues were told to quietly drop what they were doing and review surveillance video from the conference. Their job was to search the sea of protestors for familiar faces, particularly anyone from an AIDS group that received CDC funding. Once identified, those individuals were to have their funding lapse, just for booing a government official.

I couldn't believe this vindictive abuse of power. HIV was our enemy, not the vocal activist groups who were out on the streets every day performing essential AIDS services. Defunding them would only hurt the communities they served.

The time had come to re-evaluate my situation. I was now on the other side of 50. My girls had grown into fine young women and had graduated from college. Ilse was 21 and Marisa was 23. I still had a lot to offer, and after almost twenty years at CDC, I was ready for a change, although

NAVIGATING CHANGE

I still loved the CDC and its mission. But plenty of other high-profile organizations fought AIDS. One of the biggest, the Joint United Nations Programme on AIDS (UNAIDS), had shown interest in me. My experience at setting up AIDS field offices around the world had put me on their radar.

When Bush won a second term, I knew I couldn't spend another four years under this administration. I called UNAIDS the day after the 2004 election and accepted their offer. My new job would be based at the United Nations in Geneva, Switzerland. I prepared to pack up my Atlanta home and move abroad for the first time. I planned to live in France—which was a dream come true.

Thai-sponsored orphanage specializing in children who are victims of sex and human trafficking, Pattaya, Thailand, 2005.

10

WORLD STAGE

Every great dream begins with a dreamer: Always remember you have within you the strength, the patience, and the passion to reach for the stars to change the world.
- Harriet Tubman

On my third day in my new job at UNAIDS in Geneva, my wonderful new boss, Paul Delay, handed me an airplane ticket for Rome with a wry smile on his face, knowing he was throwing me in the deep end but trusting I could swim. The Vatican needed technical assistance on HIV prevention policy. I was sent there along with my colleague Sally, a world-class UNAIDS expert on faith-based organizations, for a three-day meeting. During this meeting, Roman Catholic Church leadership would decide on HIV policy for their roughly 1 billion members.

I soon learned there was even more at stake. The Vatican opposition to birth control had sparked some very public disagreements with UNAIDS, at times pitting church leaders against scientists such as Peter Piot, the organization's current executive director, over condom use—the most effective available weapon against the spread of HIV. The essential relationship between these two entities was in dire need of repair. They hoped that, as a fresh face, I might help mend some fences.

As I boarded the airplane with my colleague, a knot cinched in my stomach. I had never been to the Vatican, except once briefly as a tourist. My impressions of Catholicism, formed during childhood, had not changed in decades. I thought back to the CCD incident, when a nun tossed me out of class for speaking my mind. I also remembered my brief stint at a Catholic women's college, where I argued with my professors and got into trouble for breaking curfew. To me, the Roman Catholic Church was an ancient monolith—large, powerful, and inflexible.

We arrived in Vatican City, a tiny nation unto itself, filled with inspiring architecture and manicured gardens. A receptionist led us down a polished marble corridor to the interior meeting chambers. As I entered, the knot in my stomach tightened. Catholicism had faded from my life so long ago, yet somehow I still felt reverence for this holy place and the people in it. I pictured a room of stern priests and scowling nuns, chastising me about the evils of birth control.

Reality proved far different. Our hosts were welcoming, cordial, and genuinely interested in what we had to say. They belonged to the Vatican's Carmelite Order, tasked with developing the Church's health-related policies, including official messages about HIV/AIDS prevention and condoms.

The depth of their knowledge on these issues impressed me, as did their insightful questions.

"I must confess," I said to one of the nuns during a coffee break, "I came here with a preconceived notion of what to expect, and I was way off. The dialogue is so thoughtful and comprehensive."

She smiled knowingly, as if she had heard similar comments in the past.

The group grappled with Church doctrine on birth control and the obvious need for condoms to prevent disease transmission. They delved into situational ethics, such as condom use by a married couple when one partner is HIV positive. Everyone in the room recognized the need for a balanced, circumspect condom message as part of the Church's comprehensive policy on HIV/AIDS prevention and care. I found their conversation far more open and pragmatic than the Bush administration rhetoric shaping U.S. policy on HIV at the time.

The Sisters of the Carmelite Order, in particular, grasped the pitfalls and how to avoid them. Their male colleagues simply wanted to issue a Church-wide statement, or encyclical, but the nuns encouraged a more horizontal and inclusive strategy. A mandate would be of little use to the Church's frontline workers, who needed practical, flexible guidance. I knew this to be true from my visits to Puerto

Rico, where priests were handing out condoms. They still preached abstinence on Sundays, but the rest of the week they did what was necessary to keep people alive. The final meeting session ended, and on the way out I spotted a small, secluded chapel. I had no desire to return to the faith, but at this particular moment I did feel a need to pray. I slipped inside the chapel and sat in a pew, then knelt on the hard, wooden kneeler that reminded me of childhood. I prayed for the nuns I had met, who were making a difference in this most male-dominated of environments. I also prayed for the Puerto Rican priests, who had found the courage to rise above religious dogma for the sake of their flock.

In the chapel's stillness, I realized I needed to get better at keeping an open mind. The Roman Catholic Church had caused many problems during its long history, including the worldwide sexual-abuse scandal that was still making headlines. But there was plenty of good here, too. The meeting participants were committed to developing the best HIV policy they could. All around the world, Catholic hospitals and relief services provided invaluable care to countless people living with HIV/AIDS (Note: people living with HIV/AIDS prefer not to be called victims, as it disempowers them and does not reflect their sense of agency to help themselves). As with most things human, the Church could be viewed neither as black nor white, but a kaleidoscope of gray. Since then, I've learned to avoid preconceptions, especially when walking into a new

NAVIGATING CHANGE

situation. Sometimes people will surprise you, so it's always best to go in with an open mind and really listen and learn from what they have to say.

After returning from Rome, I began settling into my new home in the beautiful Jura Mountains of France. From those windows I could see Lake Geneva shimmer in the distance, and the ever-inspiring snow-capped peak of Mont Blanc in the French Alps beyond.

One morning during my first month I awoke to a snowstorm, and when I stepped outside my leg sank to the knee. I sure wasn't in Atlanta anymore! It snowed for four days and four nights straight, forcing me to work from home for a week (which of course I totally enjoyed) until the snowplows could clear a lane and the long driveway to my house. Not an uncommon experience living in the mountains, I would soon learn.

I had rented a large villa and asked my friend and colleague Greet, who was engaging in global HIV/AIDS work in Geneva through Tulane University, if she would like to join me. Fortunately she said yes. We both loved hiking the mountains, weekend adventures exploring the French and Swiss countryside, shopping at fresh food markets, and cooking, which, OK I admit, she was better at than me. Even though she was Belgian, she enjoyed helping me co-host traditional American Thanksgiving and Christmas dinner parties, as long as she could include a sample of Belgian beers, Belgian speculoos, and Belgian chocolates for dessert.

NAVIGATING CHANGE

Grateful friends always enjoyed leaving the city to attend one of our feasts. And for many international colleagues, a traditional American Thanksgiving dinner was a real treat.

During my first time hosting an American Thanksgiving dinner in France I was met with culture shock at every turn. First starting at the French butcher shop in my neighboring village of Divonne, where I had ordered a famous French Bourg-en-Bresse turkey weeks earlier. When I arrived, I patiently stood in line. Finally, it was my turn. I approached and told the butcher my name "Je m'appelle Madame Rugg." And in the best French accent I could muster, I said, "J'aimerais ramasser ma dinde, s'il vous plait" (I would like to pick up my turkey, please). "Oui madame," he said, and scurried to the back to get my turkey. Nothing could have prepared me for what happened next. When he came back and handed me my turkey, I screamed! It was a dead turkey all right, freshly killed, with its head, neck, feet, insides, and all its feathers still perfectly intact . . . just like the French prefer it, I later found out. I regained my composure and tried to ask as diplomatically as I could, using my limited French and silly hand gestures, for him to pluck all the feathers out of the bird and prepare it for cooking. He looked totally confused. It was quite a hilarious sight for all the French people watching in line behind me, and they started laughing.

The kind lady right behind me fortunately took pity on me and figured out what I wanted and explained it to the

NAVIGATING CHANGE

butcher. He looked really annoyed and dismayed. But she talked him into doing what I had asked for. He told me gruffly to come back in a couple hours. So I politely said, "Merci beaucoup monsieur," and went off to a lovely village cafe. I came back promptly in two hours. My turkey was ready and the butcher handed it to me politely as if everything was back to normal. I walked out of that butcher shop grinning from ear to ear, so proud of my accomplishment and becoming more French every day . . . but also laughing at the spectacle I had made of myself.

My real faux pas was that the French, of course, don't celebrate Thanksgiving, or eat turkey in November. For them, turkey is a Christmas meal. Having picked it up in early November, my turkey was still a youngin'! Mon dieu! I flew like a flash to the CarreFour, the large local supermarket with imported foods, to buy cooked turkey breasts and turkey gravy to supplement our wimpy turkey. This would be only the first of many hilarious cultural misunderstandings and missteps I would make.

I vowed to learn the language and the culture as fast as I could. The next day I sought permission to attend a renowned one month immersion course in the South of France. In the meantime, I signed up for weekly French language classes during my two-hour French lunches and focused on making new French friends.

My family often visited. Once while looking out over the scenery, my sister, Sue, and on another visit my step-sister,

Linda, both commented, "It must be a real struggle to leave such a beautiful setting every morning!" And they were right, it was. But working for UNAIDS was a dream job, and despite the steep learning curve, I woke up every morning ready to tackle it.

As the largest bureaucracy on earth, the UN moved at a glacial pace, hamstrung by endless rules and regulations. Yet during a crisis, which could spring up at any moment, you had to be ready for lightning-fast action. Demands from governments around the world, all with their own viewpoints, further complicated matters. And finally, there were the cultural differences among UN employees. I was a team leader in Monitoring and Evaluation (M&E), and every person on my team hailed from a different country. The diversity exposed us to new ways of thinking, which was wonderful, albeit sometimes challenging. But I always knew I could count on them.

No one exists in a vacuum, and a lot of my CDC and UNAIDS accomplishments were really the result of team efforts of many people too numerous to list. But particular credit goes first to my longtime friend and collaborator, Dr. Greet Peersman, who over the years cheered me on when I needed it most, using her wonderful sense of humor, which she also used when challenging me and showing me my blindspots. In both cases she helped me strengthen and flesh out my visions for better national HIV M&E systems, M&E Reference Group (MERG) normative guidelines on

NAVIGATING CHANGE

HIV prevention evaluation, and innovative approaches to international trainings. She not only enriched my thinking but enriched my life.

Credit also goes to my lifelong friend and colleague, Dr. Brazey DeZalduondo, whose humanity, unwavering support, intellectual curiosity, and challenges always helped me crystallize ideas, feel confident and energized. As an anthropologist, there was always such "synergy" when we worked together, starting out at CDC, throughout our UNAIDS days, and then beyond, emphasizing the critical role of the social and behavioral sciences in comprehensive HIV prevention policies.

I will also always remember the shared vision of a world without AIDS and the collaborative spirit and uplifting support of my dear late colleague Dr. Aristides Barbosa, Jr., the CDC Brazil Director. Aristides helped shape the history of the response to AIDS in Brazil, establish a national monitoring and evaluation system, and develop a highly successful innovative training program in Brazil, the Caribbean, and beyond.

Slowly, with the help of my colleagues, I learned to navigate the obstacles and settle into a comfortable routine. On difficult days I would come home and burn off my frustration with a brisk walk on a forest trail. If it was summer it was truly refreshing. In winter, snowshoes were often required, and it was a real workout. I really enjoyed my job; it matched my skills, interests, and talents well, and I felt I was truly making a difference.

These years in France, next to the years raising my daughters, were among the happiest in my life, both personally and professionally. I felt I was right where I belonged. I missed my girls and family, but they all visited often. Ilse, who was at that time interested in international affairs, had won a Global Young Leaders Award and traveled to Europe to participate in the model UN sessions on UN peacekeeping. And in 2010 while visiting me, she was invited to serve as a research intern at UNAIDS, helping review and analyze AIDS policy data and the infographics for the Global AIDS Report. Marisa also enjoyed visiting and would often bring her friends and future husband, using my place as a base to explore Europe.

View of Mont Blanc, French Alps, the highest mountain in Europe from my villa in Echenevex, French Jura Mountains 2005.

NAVIGATING CHANGE

My rural mountain villa in the Jura Mountains village of Echenevex, France, where I lived from October 2005-August 2011.

My mountain villa in summer, Echenevex, France, while working at UNAIDS, 2005-2011.

Hosting my first French dinner with (l-r) Greet, Matthew, Brazey, Rand, me, Paul, Karen, Steve & Cheryl, Echenevex, 2006.

UNAIDS friends at my villa (l-r) Brazey, Craig & Mary, Paul & Karen, Leo, Helena, & me- Thanksgiving dinner, Nov. 2010.

Me and Aristides Barbosa, CDC Brazil Global AIDS Program director during visit to Geneva, Switzerland, December, 2010.

Ilse participating in the Model UN Youth Leaders Summit at the Global Young Leaders Program in Geneva and Vienna.

11

MAKING A DIFFERENCE

All changes, even the most longed for, have their melancholy; for what we leave behind us is a part of ourselves.
- Anatole France

Years earlier, in the midst of twin crises at home and in my career, I had known what it was to feel disconnected from my work. Now, with my life in seemingly perfect order, I thrived at my job. Even better, humanity was finally making great strides against HIV. I had helped strengthen and manage the UNAIDS M&E Field Advisers program with key personnel placed in over 66 countries so we could help countries evaluate their progress. Then, in 2007, my boss received a promotion, and I took over for him as director of M&E.

My new role placed me at the helm of a critical new project—the Global AIDS Reporting System and Global Database. When finished, it would be the largest collection of AIDS data the world had ever seen. Our system would form the basis of UN Secretary General Global Reports on

AIDS progress. With time, it also became the premier place to go for the latest AIDS facts and figures. Researchers and government officials from around the world stayed informed by consulting our M&E system.

The streamlined M&E system became one of the strongest and most necessary functions of the UNAIDS Secretariat. It had been built on a rock-solid foundation of trust with our partners, and, as a result, 187 of the 193 UN member states were now reporting complete data in a timely manner. The system needed constant maintenance to stay in top form, and understandably I protected it like a mother bear with her cub. So, I became uneasy when a new boss showed up and began tinkering. He and I disagreed on almost everything, from handling minor maintenance issues to making big picture improvements for the future.

I came to realize that he wanted to wrestle the reins from me and put his own mark on the M&E system. I felt that while he was very bright and experienced, he saw the system I had built while leading the UNAIDS M&E Reference Group (MERG) not as a tool against AIDS, but as a self-promotion career-advancement tool. It became apparent that he also had a hard time dealing with strong, independent women like me and would try to marginalize me as a way to manage insecurity.

Unfortunately the situation deteriorated to the point where I felt totally undervalued and disrespected. It was heartbreaking. I had invested six years of my life in the

NAVIGATING CHANGE

MERG, the global M&E system, and the M&E Field Adviser Program, caring deeply about the well-being and success of each and every one of our 66 M&E field advisers in troubled countries around the world. We had shaped it into the critical monitoring and evaluation tool in the global response to HIV.

Early in my career, I learned the power of persistence, stubbornly forging through dark times until the sun shined once more. But at 58, I held a more nuanced understanding of persistence. In some instances, simply forging ahead didn't work. Staying at UNAIDS would only guarantee me further misery. I refused to accept that grim future. Instead, I would build a new future for myself somewhere else.

I learned of a vacancy at UN Secretariat headquarters in New York City. The secretary general, Mr. Ban Ki-moon, needed a new director for the Inspection and Evaluation Division. This division evaluated the efficiency and effectiveness of 33 programs and agencies, including UN Peacekeeping Operations. The division's director kept member states informed on how well, or how poorly, these agencies were meeting their objectives.

A job like that would be a huge step up from my current responsibilities. It also meant that, for the first time in 30 years, I no longer would be fighting AIDS, at least not directly. I set aside my fears that I would miss AIDS terribly and applied for the position. Then, late one night while I was on assignment, evaluating HIV prevention in drug

NAVIGATING CHANGE

users in Hanoi, Vietnam, the phone in my hotel room rang. It was the hotel operator saying the UN Secretariat in New York was calling. I waited anxiously. It was the OIOS undersecretary general Carmen Lapointe calling to inform me that I had gotten the job and to confirm my acceptance. I said, "I would be absolutely honored and delighted to accept." She then said, "I was wondering if you would be able to start fairly soon, say within the next month or two?"

I told her I would have to talk to UNAIDS but thought I could manage it. I was so excited that I didn't sleep a wink that night. Fortunately, it was the last day of my mission and I could just sleep on the long flight back to Geneva. As I dozed off, I fantasized what it would feel like to be living in New York City and working at the top of the UN.

Back in Geneva, I handed my boss my resignation letter. He didn't seem terribly surprised; he knew how dissatisfied I was. His expression only changed when he learned of my new position, which had a higher grade than his own. Suddenly his face brightened, and he became much more friendly toward me. He suggested we meet for dinner during his next visit to New York. He had shown his stripes again.

Once more I'd be moving, and this move would involve quite a lifestyle change. I'd be trading the sleepy, snow covered Jura Mountains for fast-paced Midtown Manhattan. Instead of a sprawling villa that overlooked Lake Geneva, I'd be living in a tiny, one-bedroom apartment with a view of the East River across from the UN.

NAVIGATING CHANGE

My new role would provide diplomatic status and enable me to evaluate massive, high-stakes programs and find avenues to improvement. UN Peacekeeping Operations alone spent $8 billion dollars per year to protect civilians in war-torn regions. I'd be working with ambassadors and diplomats on vital issues that affected millions of people, maybe even billions.

As I packed up the villa, I set aside my dog-eared copy of Madeleine Albright's Madam Secretary. I could imagine no better way to ready myself for the world of global politics than with a reread of this heroic woman's memoir.

Me and my boss Paul Delay launching the first UNAIDS M&E Adviser Retreat & Training October, 2006, in Glion, Switzerland.

UNAIDS M&E Field Advisers at first global training at UNAIDS headquarters in Geneva and Glion, Switzerland, 2006.

Dr. Peter Piot, UNAIDS Executive Director 1994-2009, Bangladesh M&E Adviser Dr Mahboop & me, M&E training, Glion 2006.

February 2011, Geneva- Me and the UNAIDS M&E Reference Group (MERG) members at my last meeting as Chair.

AIDS education outreach with a local market vendor, Hanoi, Vietnam discussing HIV risk among villagers, 2011.

Vietnam 2011- HIV worker demonstrates needle exchange dropbox. Users drop used needles and get clean syringes & condoms.

NAVIGATING CHANGE

Me on the Ha Long Bay, Vietnam, during a U.S. Institute of Medicine Scientific Review Committee site visit, April, 2011.

View of floating markets and brothels on Ha Long Bay, Gulf of Tonkin, Vietnam during site visit for the US IOM Apr 2011.

12

ART OF DIPLOMACY

It took me quite a long time to develop a voice, and now that I have it, I am not going to be silent. - Madeleine Albright

The next chapter of my life was going to be a hard pivot. I was leaving my 30-year career fighting the AIDS pandemic in the global health sector to engage in a higher and more political platform, which is the UN Headquarters Secretariat in New York. I made the decision to make this pivot and leave AIDS behind, not only because it was a promotion, but because the time was right and I could stay true to my core goal of devoting my life to helping make a better world, especially for those less fortunate in the developing world. It just felt right. Although I was scared and anxious about starting over in this new place where I didn't know anyone, missing all of my good friends and colleagues from my days fighting AIDS for over 30 years, I was ready for a change. In my heart I realized the universe was once again nudging me to pursue this new path.

NAVIGATING CHANGE

During this transition, I learned a lot about myself. I learned that my life's callings were going to take many forms depending on the times; that it's OK to leave one sector if your core values are still being served; that each step you take into fear will strengthen you and help you confront future fears with poise, courage, and confidence. When I saw the heights of accomplishments and the personal evolution I had attained by walking through my fears, my faith in myself grew.

I also came to understand how important it is to figure out what is really essential to you and what drives you. For me it was being a leader, and by now I knew I was a leader at my core. This new job would be a fabulous opportunity to really challenge myself with new levels of responsibility and grow my leadership skills at the top of the UN.

I would advise anyone struggling to make decisions about their own career to realize that life is going to take you in a lot of different directions. You have to stay true to yourself, true to your core values and life goals, and find people who will help you learn the ropes as you go and who truly inspire you.

Madeleine Albright was that kind of inspiration for me. Like me, she had built her life on a bedrock of education, earning a PhD from Columbia before joining the faculty at Georgetown. An expert in foreign policy, she advised Washington politicians and then became U.S. ambassador to the United Nations. She held that position until 1997,

NAVIGATING CHANGE

when President Bill Clinton made her his secretary of state. I admired Albright's achievements, but more than that, her style. This slight woman knew how to maneuver, quite successfully, in the domain of powerful men. I had dedicated my career to helping people in need and always worked to reach a larger stage so I could help more people. Madeleine Albright had reached the pinnacle by wielding her authority for the greater good, which to me was the only path worth following. Inspired by these thoughts, I walked onto the UN main campus for my first day on the job.

It was like walking into a minefield. The UN General Assembly was in session when I arrived, so the campus buzzed with activity. I had expected an orientation period, where I could settle into my office and learn the job, but instead I found myself in high-level meetings right away. Worse, my reception from the member states was far less than warm. At every meeting, it seemed delegates grilled and harangued me. I couldn't understand why.

I went home to my tiny apartment and stood at the window, absently watching sailboats move along the East River. What had I gotten myself into? How would I survive in such a hostile workplace? I didn't know the answers, but my respect for Madeleine Albright reached new heights. I took a deep breath, finding an inner calm. She had figured this place out, and so would I.

Each day, as difficult as it was, I steeled myself and went back into the minefield. Gradually, the map of hidden landmines revealed itself to me. I was a technical person working in a highly political environment. International politics, particularly, had a lot of moving parts. The attacks on me weren't personal, I realized. They were just another example of everyday business at the UN. My U.S. nationality, my role as an evaluator (people always felt I'd be judging their performance), and a variety of other factors all played a part. Clearly, I'd need to cultivate new political skills before I could thrive here.

I would also need to win over my staff in the Inspection and Evaluation Division. My vision of evaluation involved more of a collaborative approach and learning model. This differed from the environment established by the first director, who focused evaluation solely as an accountability function. While holding people accountable can be an aspect of any evaluation, I believe the real value of evaluation is in helping people, programs, and systems LEARN how to become more effective, adaptive, coherent, sustainable, and successful. I encouraged my evaluation staff to include a learning and research translation phase at the end of every study to help program management understand, learn, and translate results into actions. We conducted nine evaluations per year in areas such as the environment, drugs and crime, refugees, and humanitarian relief. We would then conduct progress reviews three years later to learn if our recommendations were making a difference.

NAVIGATING CHANGE

Once we got rolling, the evaluations proceeded at a lightning pace. I worked late into the evening. Some nights I'd come home and walk straight to the bedroom, collapsing on the bed and falling into a deep sleep. I'd wake up early the next morning ready to do it all over again.

The time came to evaluate UN Peacekeeping Operations. This one, I knew, would be a challenge because of its complexity and political implications. Peacekeepers had a mandate to protect civilians, with force when warranted, but it was very nuanced, and any failure would reflect poorly on the UN. Still, the evaluation had to be done and my courageous staff and team leaders were committed to seeing it through. We began conducting site visits and reviewing incident reports.

Our findings painted a bleak picture. In too many instances, peacekeepers were failing to protect civilians, even when the use of force was clearly warranted. Their command structure formed the root of the problem. Since my father and brothers were military men, I knew something about command-and-control structures. You need a well-established chain of command so that, during an emergency, resources can be deployed quickly and effectively. Only a single leader, or a tight group of leaders, can act so decisively.

Peacekeepers, unfortunately, were operating under a decentralized command structure. A nation that contributed troops continued to maintain control over its units, which sounded fine in principle but caused major problems in a crisis. The peacekeepers needed to obtain their country's approval before carrying out the UN commander's orders. This unwieldy process caused delays when swift action was needed to save lives. Sometimes countries actually instructed their units to stand down, leaving the UN commander shorthanded during an emergency.

Our evaluations revealed something even more disturbing. In some instances, peacekeepers were sexually exploiting and abusing the people they were supposed to protect. We uncovered cases of peacekeepers trading money and goods for sex, or sometimes doing worse, and then going unpunished because of their diplomatic immunity. We recommended that UN troop commanders be held accountable for the actions of their peacekeepers and that those proved negligent be relieved of their commission.

The evaluation results made waves within the UN, with some member states demanding changes to peacekeeping operations and others remaining stubbornly intransigent. Then The New York Times and some European press agencies got hold of the report. In the past, the media might never have learned of our findings. But something special had recently occurred: our evaluation division, like the audit division, had received permission in 2014 to start posting our reports directly to the UN website, where previously they would not have been available to the public. It was a huge win for proponents of public transparency like me.

NAVIGATING CHANGE

Once the public learned of ongoing peacekeeper sexual exploitation and abuse, the UN secretary general had no choice but to act. Commanding officers could now lose their commission if such crimes occurred on their watch. Our evaluations were having an impact. Unfortunately, the UN Security Council and Peacekeeping Operations failed to change the decentralized command structure, which to me and others remains as inefficient and potentially dangerous as ever.

By now, the benefits of evaluating UN programs and agencies had become obvious, but many delegates still casually dismissed my division and our work. In addition to my full-time job as director, I also chaired the UN Evaluation Group (UNEG), an interagency network of evaluation leaders dedicated to good governance and oversight of the UN system. As chair of UNEG I worked with the World Bank, the Organization for Economic Cooperation and Development's Development Assistance Committee in Paris, and professional evaluation groups, such as Evalpartners and the American Evaluation Association (AEA). I served on the AEA Board of Directors and as the international section co-editor for the American Journal of Evaluation.

We decided that the best way to promote our cause would be to catalyze a UN General Assembly resolution on evaluation and designate 2015 as the International Year of Evaluation. The UN resolution would call for strengthening the necessary capacity of countries to conduct their own evaluations so they could be in the driver's seat.

The goal was to reduce countries' reliance on external international evaluators parachuting in, conducting an evaluation, and leaving with the data for the global donors who hired them, such as the World Bank, without sharing it with local governments. This would also help countries use evaluation tools and not be so afraid of them. If they could own it, design it, and conduct it, they could decide how to use the results. This resolution was intended to empower countries and help reduce the fear and misperceptions surrounding evaluation. We needed to change the negative connotation, expressed succinctly by developing country ambassadors who said from their experiences "evaluation's purpose is for donors to decide whose funding to cut." No wonder people fear it.

Convincing a majority of nations to agree on anything can be challenging. In our case, it would be especially difficult. Right from the start, I knew we'd be climbing a mountain of fear, misperception, and confusion. I also knew that, as the UNEG chair, it would fall on me to do much of the educating and lobbying.

As always, the key was finding a strong ally, which in this case turned out to be the senior representative from Ireland, Mr. Vincent Herlihy. There were others, to be sure, but Vincent became a true outspoken champion for evaluation. He understood the barriers to getting a stand-alone resolution on evaluation through the General Assembly. The first thing we did was recruit like-minded delegates and invite them to informal breakfasts and lunches to brainstorm.

Vincent encouraged us to think strategically at every turn. Meanwhile, he worked behind the scenes, trying to garner more support for the resolution and developed an informal Friends of Evaluation Group. Often he would contact my assistants, Laura and Sonila, to arrange impromptu meetings for me and UNEG colleagues to speak with delegates to answer their latest questions and concerns. As I talked, I'd see their heads nodding in agreement, and a delegate eventually would say, "OK, I will take this back to my capital and see if we can support it."

Sometimes we'd hear rumors of an attempt to kill the resolution. Clearly, we needed an advocate from a developing country, someone who'd show the others they had nothing to fear. After knocking on many doors, one influential insider agreed to stick out his neck. Ambassador Peter Thompson of Fiji was a successful businessman before becoming a UN ambassador and had decided to take up the environmental fight on behalf of his small island and other island states. As the oceans changed, small island nations were the first to feel the effects, like canaries in a mineshaft. Peter realized that we couldn't protect the environment, especially the world's oceans, without good evaluation.

During the closing months of 2014, the Missions of Fiji, Ireland, their allies, and I with my UNEG colleagues made one final push for support, enlisting 43 countries to stand up for our resolution. I barely slept at all in those final weeks, and then the big day arrived when the General Assembly voted on our Resolution 69/237. I felt guardedly optimistic that we had enough votes, but I was unprepared for what happened next—the resolution passed almost unanimously.

Thanks to a tireless team effort by all stakeholders, the entire General Assembly had agreed to the resolution on strengthening the national evaluation capacities for member countries' own development activities, authorizing UN agencies to provide the support needed upon request, and recognizing 2015 as the International Year of Evaluation. It was one of the proudest moments of my career.

My first day on the job as Director, UN OIOS Inspection and Evaluation Division, New York, August 2011.

Conducting humanitarian needs focus group with my UN teammate Juan Carlos and the villagers near Rangoon, Myanmar, 2012.

Giving a speech on UN TV on importance and need for the new evaluation resolution, UN HQ, New York, 2013.

UN Evaluation Week 2013: Michel Sidibe, UNAIDS Director; me; Ugandan official; Carmen Lapointe, USG OIOS; Nick York, UK.

NAVIGATING CHANGE

The Power of Evaluation the United Nations

A message from the Director of the Inspection and Evaluation Division (IED), Office of Internal Oversight Services (OIOS) at the United Nations

As IED Director & UNEG Chair, I held meetings to strengthen evaluation at the UN, including UN Peacekeeping, NY, 2014.

UN resolution ceremony(l-r) Navid, Vincent, Carmen, Scott, Kristinn, me, Marco, Peter, Colin, Peni, Andrea, Indran, 2014

NAVIGATING CHANGE

UN Secretary General Ban Ki-moon & me upon my retirement, UN Secretariat, New York, March, 2015.

13

TAKING A NEW TACK

> *There is much monitoring, but very little evaluation . . . Evaluation should be seen as the centerpiece of the learning process. - Amina Mohammed, UN Deputy Secretary General, speech on the need for evaluation in the 2030 Agenda for Sustainable Development, March 2015*

This landmark resolutions near unanimous endorsement felt like a turning point. At last, the UN had recognized evaluation as a right, like free speech or gender equality. Citizens have a right to know that their government's programs are effective, like consumers have the right to know the products they consume are safe. It is the moral imperative of governments and corporations alike to provide this transparent information. Thus citizens are entitled to hold their governments accountable. Furthermore, if you believe that safety and security are rights, then it follows that evaluation is a right as well, because in our global society, you cannot have one without the other; you cannot ensure safety or security without thorough methodical evaluation. It seemed we had reached a new understanding, a new era at the UN.

Unfortunately, the long entrenched, politics-as-usual mindset refused to yield so easily. Developing countries from the Global South continued to oppose evaluation, feeling it was a form of accountability held only by the Global North over countries in the Global South. This would be an even higher stakes political mountain to climb as the UN negotiated its most ambitious global initiative ever, the new 2030 Agenda for Sustainable Development to address the universal top 17 Sustainable Development Goals (SDGs) for all countries in the world. The SDGs, which included ambitious targets like zero poverty and hunger, quality education for all, and worldwide gender equality, were set to be voted on by all 193 countries in the General Assembly in September 2015.

Meanwhile it came to pass that I was facing mandatory retirement because I would soon be 62. This meant I wouldn't be able to join the fight . . . or at least that is what I thought in March 2015.

I had learned long ago that setbacks could be a springboard to success. Every morning on my way to work, I walked past the U.S. Mission to the United Nations on First Avenue at East 45th Street. It was an imposing sight, with floor to-ceiling windows that revealed a stylish interior of art and sculpture. A week before I was about to retire,

NAVIGATING CHANGE

while walking past this grand building completely uncertain about my future, I had an idea.

The United States, as the largest donor country in the world, had a natural interest in evaluation. Americans deserved to know if all those billions of tax dollars spent on foreign aid were making an impact. So, I sent out feelers to the U.S. Mission, asking if they would be interested in having a senior evaluation consultant on their SDG team. They leapt at the chance. Within two weeks, I was working as a consultant for the U.S. Mission to the UN. Again I felt like the universe had my back.

My first day at this job felt different than the others. No longer did I feel like an outsider entering a strange, unfamiliar world. As I stood in the inner lobby, waiting to be escorted to the higher floors, I looked up and saw a huge plaque with the name Madeline Albright in gold letters. It filled me with joy. This was where she had worked as U.S. secretary of state 14 years earlier. This was where I had always fantasized about working, and now I was quite literally walking in her footsteps. I felt instantly that I belonged.

At the time, all of the UN was engaged in finalizing its three-year negotiation process to produce globally agreed upon Sustainable Development Goals, or SDGs. These goals, to be achieved by the year 2030, offered the world a better and more sustainable future. My role was to help make sure a clear evaluation framework and language was included, encouraging countries to evaluate success in achieving their national SDG and voluntarily reporting at the UN High Level Political Forums.

My UN experience told me it would be a struggle, and indeed it was. But this effort would differ from those earlier efforts in one significant way: This time, my colleagues and I had the full weight of the United States government behind us. This was when Barack Obama was U.S. President, John Kerry was Secretary of State, and Samantha Power was U.S. Ambassador to the UN. I worked as a strategic adviser on the SDG team supporting Samantha. My former UN allies were happy to sign on for this battle as well, and evaluation featured prominently in their opening statements on the floor of the General Assembly. From that moment on, I knew we would succeed.

When the battle finally ended, I received a note from my U.S. Mission team leader, Tony Pipa. It read, in part, "If not for your presence, tactful pressure, and continuous efforts, we would not have gotten evaluation as a guiding principle into the new 2030 Agenda for Sustainable Development. Thank you." I smiled as I almost cried, welling up inside with a deep sense of accomplishment. It was the crowning achievement of my 28 years in public service.

Countries around the globe would soon be embarking on a 15-year mission to meet the newly established SDGs. Evaluation would be their yardstick for success, and someone needed to train all those leaders in evaluation. So in 2016, I established the Claremont Evaluation Center–

NAVIGATING CHANGE

New York (CEC–NY) across the street from the UN with support from Claremont Graduate University, which had just hired me as a professor in the School of Social Science, Policy, and Evaluation. Less than a year later, we offered a very successful international course newly developed by a team that included myself, Micheal Quinn Patton (founder of Utilization-focused Evaluation, a global gold standard), Zenda Ofir, John Gargani, and Claremont colleagues Stewart Donaldson, Michelle Bligh, Tarek Azzam, Nina Sabarre, and Omara Turner.

I was still happily living and working in New York when COVID-19 exploded around the planet in a matter of weeks. On March 10, 2020, for the first time in history, the UN shuttered its doors and sent all staff home to figure out the new world of remote working and virtual meetings.

The epidemiologist in me tracked the virus with professional detachment at first, but then, quite suddenly, it became personal. I watched in horror as the disease swept through New York City like a tsunami. Bustling streets suddenly became barren, and Manhattan became a ghost town, punctuated only by sirens and the constant round-the-clock parade of ambulances, police cars, and firetrucks which continued constantly, day and night, as things got worse. Living between two major hospitals, whenever I ventured outside for groceries or a necessary bit of fresh air and some exercise, I would pass the horrifying site of refrigerated trucks that had been pressed into service as emergency morgues.

It was apocalyptic and emotionally scarring. The only saving grace came each night at 7 p.m. when New Yorkers everywhere leaned out of their windows and with full hearts, banged pots and pans and cheered loudly for all the doctors, nurses, and frontline workers starting and finishing their shifts. Sometimes I was out walking alone and close enough, though masked, to see the exhaustion in their eyes. During this darkest of times it was reassuring to witness that familiar resilience; the spirit of New Yorkers could be felt, seen, and heard every night.

As time went on, I felt the overwhelming urge to be near my family. The initial surge of cases abated, but I knew it was just a temporary reprieve. I decided to pack up my belongings, eventually sell my apartment, and move cross country in the middle of a pandemic.

I was heading back to where it all began.

Me & Amina Mohammed, UN Deputy Secretary General supporting inclusion of Evaluation in the SDGs, New York, August, 2015.

The United Nations' 17 Universal Sustainable Development Goals (SDGs) were unanimously adopted in September 2015 in New York.

UN Claremont Evaluation Center-New York brochure- "The place for strategic global leadership in evaluation", Oct 2016.

NAVIGATING CHANGE

UN General Assembly podium with Claremont Evaluation Center-NY colleagues (l-r) John, Nina, me, Tarek, Stewart, NY 2016.

NAVIGATING CHANGE

Me & Michael Quinn Patton, Utilization-focused Evaluation, CEC-NY Executive Leaders Evaluation Training, New York, 2017.

UN leaders attending first CEC-NY executive SDG evaluation training visit UN Security Council Chambers, New York, 2017.

NAVIGATING CHANGE

May 2018 launch of my new company, Evaluation Consultants LLC, 'taking the bull by the horns' near Wall St. in New York.

14

FULL CIRCLE

The world of the future is in our making. Tomorrow is now. - Eleanor Roosevelt

Forty years earlier, I was a PhD candidate at the University of California, San Francisco. Back then, I anticipated a quiet career in academia, until a deadly, new virus called HIV took me on an odyssey around the world. Now, another new and deadly virus brought me back. I was once more living in the Bay Area, where my girls had settled.

Returning to this place felt both strange and familiar. I walked the same streets I did four decades ago and ate in the same restaurants, but somehow, they no longer felt like mine. Time had subtly altered them, and only a few of the familiar faces of colleagues remained. I felt like a ghost. The pandemic didn't help, of course. Everyone had grown accustomed to masks and social distancing and supply-chain shortages, but we all sensed our previous world was gone, possibly forever.

NAVIGATING CHANGE

As for me, at age 65 I finally decided to become my own boss, launching a startup called Evaluation Consultants, LLC. It's been going well despite the pandemic, and our growing client list mostly includes large, international entities like UNICEF, USAID's Ebola efforts, and WHO and COVID-19-related evaluations, such as GAVI's (the Global Vaccine Alliance) global COVAX Facility Evaluation. As with any new venture there are plenty of challenges, but I've enjoyed taking the helm and making the tough calls. It's a transformative chapter in my life, and my passion to make a difference in the world still drives me.

In my personal life I've taken up sailing, going out on the San Francisco Bay each weekend for regattas and races. Speeding across the water feels a lot like flying, which is probably why I'm so drawn to it. More than once while sailing I've glanced to the sky and remembered that crystal blue day over Wisconsin, when Dad handed me control of the Cessna. I wish he could see me now.

My decision to return to San Francisco to be with family was one of the best I ever made. My daughters have built meaningful lives for themselves and I could not be prouder. I now have two adorable grandsons, Owen and Edward, to cherish as well.

Somewhere, among all the studies, outreach programs, training, activism, and evaluations, I know I made a difference and manifested my dreams. It would be nice to point to some specific sliver of human progress and claim it

NAVIGATING CHANGE

as mine, but that's not how progress works. We all contribute to the greater good, as did the generations before us. My work, in collaboration with others, has helped save lives that would have been claimed by tobacco, or HIV, or some other malady. I was able to help, at least a little, to mitigate the fear and panic that comes with a pandemic and reduce the discrimination and stigma felt by those most vulnerable and marginalized by society. Knowing that those people went on to make their own contributions to a better world is enough for me.

So as I wrap this up, I would like to offer a summary of my career advice, especially for those just starting out:

1. If you see a big gap or unmet knowledge or service need in your organization, your field, your community, or beyond, let your creativity soar and imagine the possibilities, then embrace your fears and take a chance, let these dreams spark your (entrepreneurial) spirit and start something new or start your own center within an existing structure.
2. Speak up and speak your truth, but read the room first and don't try to do it alone. Find like-minded colleagues and make them your allies. This is the essence of relationship building and the art of diplomacy.
3. If you find yourself an outsider, lead from behind the scenes by allowing powerful others to deliver your message. Soon you will be accepted as the leader you are.

NAVIGATING CHANGE

4. Recognize that unexpected setbacks can become springboards of opportunity. Life will have many unexpected events, but the universe will provide if you keep showing up.
5. If, after trying your best, you still find yourself in a bad situation, have the courage to pivot in a new direction. When considering a job change, be sure to choose your new boss carefully. They can make or break your experience.
6. Always stay true to your core values and what's really meaningful to you, knowing that this may evolve and take on different shapes over time.

I would like to close with what is for me a deeply resonant quote from Maya Angelou: "During bad circumstances, which is human inheritance, you must decide not to be reduced. You have your humanity, and you must not allow anything to reduce that. We are GLOBAL CITIZENS. Disasters remind us we are world citizens, whether we like it or not."

Never forget that you too are making a difference. It may not feel that way, as you scramble through your daily maze of responsibilities, but all that work adds up. Trust that every day you are influencing the people around you and contributing to the greater good. Someday you'll look back and realize every precious minute was time well-spent, whether it was on family or in your career. So, just keep going, putting one foot in front of the other, doing what you

NAVIGATING CHANGE

love, taking the bull by the horns, never ever giving up, and remembering, one person really can make a difference!

Ilse, me & Marisa celebrating Ilse's 30th birthday at her favorite winery in Sonoma-Napa Valley, CA, September 2, 2014.

NAVIGATING CHANGE

Ilse, Marisa and me celebrating Marisa's wedding, The Legion of Honor Museum, San Francisco, CA, September 5, 2015.

'Global Evaluation Salon', my NY apartment (l-r) Tina, Rita, Indran, Jo, me, Laura, David, Nancy, Brazey & Inga, 2019.

Flying in an amphibious seaplane over Marin and San Francisco during COVID (mask down just for a moment), August, 2021.

NAVIGATING CHANGE

Taking the helm and sailing on the San Francisco Bay... a dream come true.

DEDICATION

I would like to dedicate this book to my two beautiful, resilient and loving daughters, Marisa and Ilse, who have always been my true north and continue to provide the joy in my life.

ABOUT THE AUTHOR

Deborah Rugg, PhD, has had a distinguished career over 40 years in epidemiological and international program and policy evaluation across a variety of agencies, including CDC, UNAIDS, UN OIOS, USAID, the US Mission to the UN, UNICEF, and philanthropies. She has led research and evaluation on topics ranging from global health responses to the AIDS epidemic to health emergencies such as the Ebola outbreak of 2014-16, to the COVID-19 pandemic, leading a GAVI (Global Vaccine Alliance) - sponsored evaluation of the global vaccine equitable distribution program called the COVAX Facility. She has also led high profile evaluations of UN peacekeeping operations, of the SDGs and UN agency performance. Her leadership has been recognized by the AEA and CDC who have awarded her the Alva and Gunnar Myrdal Award for Leadership in Government Service and the CDC Award for Leadership in Advancing the Behavioral and Social Sciences.

In 2018, she formed her own company Evaluation Consultants LLC, which provides consultative services on metrics and evaluation to the private sector, philanthropies, national governments, and UN entities to strengthen evaluation at global and country levels.

NAVIGATING CHANGE

She was appointed in 2017 to the Executive Board of Directors of the American Evaluation Association and Section Co-Editor of the American Journal of Evaluation International Developments in Evaluation. In 2016 she was founding director of the Claremont Evaluation Center-New York and launched the Executive Leadership Program in Evaluation of the SDGs, while serving as a Professor at Claremont Graduate University, School of Social Science, Policy and Evaluation. In 2015, she led the charge to include evaluation principles in the UN global 2030 Agenda for Sustainable Development while serving as SDG Evaluation Adviser to the United States Mission to the UN in New York.

From 2011-2015, she served as Director, Inspection and Evaluation Division, UN OIOS and Chair of the UN Evaluation Group. She shepherded complex political processes through the UN General Assembly with the landmark UN GA Resolution on Evaluation (GA/69/237, 19 Dec 2014), which focused on building country-level capacity for evaluation and was instrumental in the UN General Assembly's recognizing 2015 as the International Year of Evaluation. From 2005-2011 she served as the Monitoring & Evaluation Director at UNAIDS in Geneva, establishing M&E Field Advisers in over 66 countries and leading the Global AIDS Reporting System. This was after completing almost 20 years at the US CDC in Atlanta, where she started as an Epidemic Intelligence Officer in 1987 and ended as the Associate Director for M&E, Global AIDS Program in

2005. She earned her PhD in Health Psychology from UCSF School of Medicine in 1982.

Deborah currently lives in Mill Valley, California and enjoys hiking, spending time with her family, and sailing on the San Francisco Bay.

SUGGESTED READINGS

Recommended YouTube Videos (which can be found by searching Deborah Rugg):

2021, June- American Evaluation Association (AEA), American Journal of Evaluation Podcast Series "International Developments in Evaluation"- Zenda Ofir & Deborah Rugg

2017- Claremont Graduate University - "The Garden View with Deborah Rugg", as Director, discusses the SDGs & launch of the Claremont Evaluation Center- NY (CEC-NY)

2015, November-Chicago- American Evaluation Association Conference Opening Plenary: "Evaluation in the SDG era, the 2015 International Year of Evaluation & the New UN Resolution on Evaluation".

2015, April-3ie Howard White Keynote lecture: "Evaluation & Politics: Tips & Barriers to Use by Deborah Rugg" -RETIREMENT speech highlighting lessons learned from over 35 years at CDC & the UN

2014, July 11- New York- UNEG "Introductory Remarks by Deborah Rugg at UNEG's High-level Event". Discusses the role of evaluation in the UN and the SDG era

2014, July 11- New York- UNEG "Closing Remarks by Deborah Rugg at UNEG's High-level Event". Discusses priorities for the future of evaluation at the UN

2014, April - Bangkok, Thailand- "ESCAP High-Level Panel Introductory Remarks by UNEG Chair Deborah Rugg". Discusses regional and global evaluation challenges

2013, March- New York- UNEG "Introductory Remarks by Deborah Rugg"- with the UN Secretary General Ban Ki-moon at UNEG Evaluation Week Special Event

2013, March- New York- UNEG Chair Deborah Rugg -"On the Importance of Evaluation"

2013, March- New York- UNEG Chair Deborah Rugg- "On the new UNEG Strategy to help improve evaluation in the UN"

Other AIDS-related memoirs:
Guinan, M. *Adventures of a female disease detective: In pursuit of smallpox and AIDS*. Baltimore, MD: Johns Hopkins University Press, 2021.

Piot, P. *AIDS: Between Science & Politics*. New York, NY: Columbia University Press, 2015.

Shilts, R. *And the band played on: Politics, people, and the AIDS epidemic*. New York, NY: St. Martin's Press, 1987.

Selected references from across my career:
Ofir, Z. & Rugg, D. (Eds) Transformational Evaluation for Times of Global Transformation, International Developments in Evaluation Section, *American Journal of Evaluation*, Vol. 42, Issue 1, 2021.

Rugg, D. The Role of Evaluation at the UN and in the Sustainable Development Goals: Towards the Future We Want. In Jean-Marc Coicaud & Juha Uitto (Eds), *Special Issue on Evaluating International Development Cooperation, Global Policy Journal*, September 2016.

Rugg, D. Evaluation and Politics: Tips and Barriers to Use of Evaluation. *International Journal of Development Evaluation*, August 2016.

Rugg, D, Hauge, A. et al. UN Thematic Evaluation of the Monitoring and Evaluation of the Millennium Development Goals: Lessons Learned for the Post-2015 Era: Report of the Office of Internal Oversight Services, published by *the UN Economic and Social Council*, New York, NY,18 March 2015.

Rugg, D. Lighting of the Torch – 2015 International Year of Evaluation. In Rugg, D. & Hauge, A. (Eds), *Inspection and Evaluation News - UN Inspection and Evaluation Division*: New York, Vol 3:1, 28 February 2015.

Laga M, Rugg D, Peersman G, & Ainsworth M. Evaluating HIV Prevention Effectiveness: The Perfect as the Enemy of the Good. *Journal of AIDS*, 26(7): 779-783, 2012.

Rugg, D., Marais, H., & Carael, M. (Eds). Progress Towards Global HIV Targets: Challenges in Monitoring National Indicators. *Journal of AIDS*, 52(Suppl2): S69-SJ59, 2009.

Rugg, D., Marais, H., Carael, M., DeLay, P., & Warner-Smith, M. Are We on Course for Reporting on the Millennium Development Goals in 2015? *Journal of AIDS*, 52(Supp12): S69-S76, 2009.

Peersman, G., Rugg, D., Erkkola, T., Kiwango, E., & Yang. Are the Investments in National HIV Monitoring and Evaluation Systems Paying Off? *Journal of AIDS*, 52 (Suppl2): S87-S96, 2009.

Rugg, D., Peersman, G., & Carael, M. (Eds.) Global Advances in HIV/AIDS Monitoring and Evaluation. *New Directions for Evaluation*, No. 103, pp.1-12, 2004.

Rugg, D., Carael, M., Boerma, T., & Novak, J. Global Advances in Monitoring and Evaluation of HIV/AIDS: From AIDS Case Reporting to Program Improvement. *New Directions for Evaluation*, No. 103, pp.33-48, 2004.

Rugg, D., Novak, J., Peersman, G., St Louis, M., Heckert, K., & Spencer, J. Efforts in Collaboration and Coordination of HIV/AIDS Monitoring and Evaluation: Contributions and Lessons of Two U.S. Government Agencies in a Global Partnership. *New Directions for Evaluation*, No.103, pp.65-80, 2004.

Rosser, B.R.S., Bockting, W., Ross, M., Rugg, D., Bauer, G., Craft, C., Robinson, B., & Coleman, E. Modifying Internalized Homonegativity in Men Who Have Sex with Men. *Health Psychology*, 2002.

Rosser, B.R.S., Bockting, W., Rugg, D., Robinson, B., Ross, M., Bauer, G., Craft, C., & Coleman, E. A Randomized Controlled Trial of Sexual Health Approach to Long-Term HIV Risk Reduction for Men Who Have Sex with Men: Effects on Unsafe Behavior. *AIDS Education and Prevention*, 2001.

Rosser, B.RS., Rugg, D. & Ross, M. Increasing Research & Evaluation Productivity: Tips for Successful Writing Retreats. *Health Promotion Practice*, Vol. 2, No.1, pp. 9-13, 2001.

Rugg, D. & Mills, S. Developing an Integrated and Comprehensive Monitoring and Evaluation Plan. In: Rehle, T., Saidel, T., Mills, S., and Magnani, R (Eds.) Evaluating Programs for HIV/AIDS Prevention and Care in Developing Countries: A Handbook for Program Managers & Decision Makers. *Family Health Internationa*l: Arlington, VA., pp. 23-32, 2001.

Rugg, D., Heitgerd, J., Cotton, D., Broyles, S., Freeman, A., Lopez-Gomez, A.M., Cotten- Oldenburg, N., Page-Shafer, K. and the HPI Field Collaborative. CDC HIV prevention indicators: Monitoring and Evaluating HIV Prevention in the USA. *AIDS*, Vol.14, No. l3, pp. 2003-2013, 2000.

Page-Shafer, K., Kim, A., Rugg, D., Norton, P., Heitgerd, J., Katz, M., & McFarland, W. Evaluating National HIV Prevention Indicators: A Case Study in San Francisco. *AIDS*, Vol. 14, No. 13, pp. 2015-2026, 2000.

Rugg, D., Buehler, J., Renaud, M., Gilliam, A, Heitgerd, J., Westover, B., Wright-DeAguero, L., Bartholow, K., & Swanson, S. Evaluating HIV Prevention: A Framework for National, State, and Local Levels. *American Journal of Evaluation*, Vol 20, No 1, pp. 35-56, 1999.

Rugg, D., Levinson, R, DiClemente, R, & Fishbein, M. CDC Partnerships with External Behavioral and Social Scientists: Roles, Extramural Funding, and Employment. *American Psychologist*, Vol. 52, No.2, Feb. 1997.

Rugg, D., Lamptey, P. & Kendall, C. Primary HIV prevention strategies. In Cohen, B. & Trussell, J. (Eds), Preventing and Mitigating AIDS in Sub-Saharan Africa: Research and Data Priorities for the Social and Behavioral Sciences, *National Research Council/ National Academy Press*, Washington, D.C., 1995.

Rugg, D. School-Based HIV Education Strategies That Work Best in Reducing Risky Sexual Behavior Among U.S. Teenagers. *In Proceedings of NIH U.S.-Israeli Binational Symposium on Adolescent Health*, Jerusalem, Israel, Acta Pediatrica, Nov 1994.

Rugg, D., MacGowan, R, Stark, K. & Swanson, N. Evaluating the CDC Program for HIV Counseling and Testing. *Public Health Reports*, Vol. 106, No.6, 708-713, 1991.

Rugg, D., O'Reilly, K. & Galavotti, C. AIDS Prevention Evaluation: Conceptual and Methodological Issues. *Evaluation & Program Planning*, Vol.13, No.1, 79-89, 1990.

Rugg, D. AIDS Prevention: A Public Health Psychology Perspective. *New Directions in Program Evaluation: A Quarterly Sourcebook*, No.46, 7-22, Summer, 1990.

Rugg, D., Hovell, M. & Franzini, L. Behavioral Science & Public Health Perspectives: Combining Paradigms for the Prevention and Control of AIDS. In Temoshok, L. & Baum, A (Eds.) *Psychological Perspectives on AIDS: Etiology, Prevention, & Treatment*. Lawrence Erlbaum Assoc: Hillsdale, New Jersey,17-34, 1990.

Story Terrace

www.ingramcontent.com/pod-product-compliance
Lightning Source LLC
LaVergne TN
LVHW061624070526
838199LV00070B/6563